AF796808

Ocracoke

In the Fifties

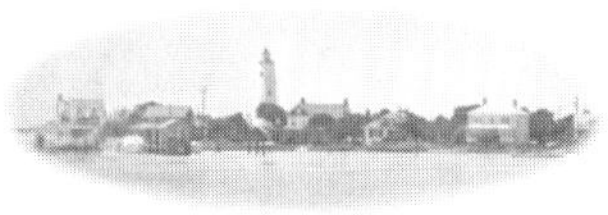

Also by Dare Wright

Lonely Doll Books

The Lonely Doll (1957)
Holiday for Edith & the Bears (1958)
The Doll and the Kitten (1960)
The Lonely Doll Learns a Lesson (1961)
Edith & Mr. Bear (1964)
A Gift from the Lonely Doll (1966)
Edith and Big Bad Bill (1968)
Edith and Little Bear Lend a Hand (1972)
Edith and Midnight (1978)
Edith and the Duckling (1981)

Other Books

The Little One (1959)
Date with London (1961)
Lona (1963)
Take Me Home (1965)
Look at a Gull (1967)
Look at a Colt (1969)
The Kitten's Little Boy (1971)
Look at a Calf (1974)
Look at a Kitten (1975)

Unpublished Manuscript

"Make Me Real"

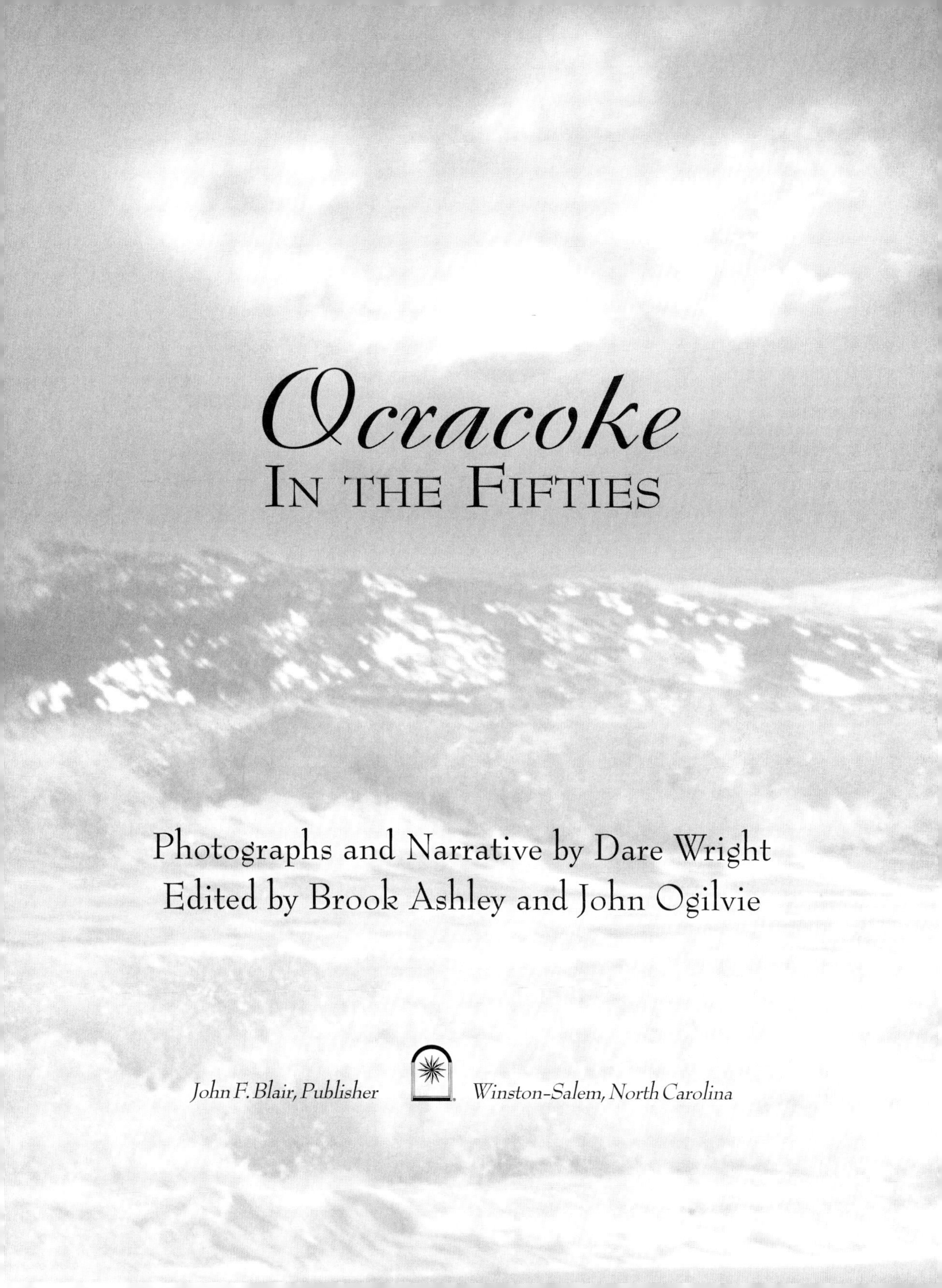

Ocracoke In the Fifties

Photographs and Narrative by Dare Wright
Edited by Brook Ashley and John Ogilvie

John F. Blair, Publisher *Winston-Salem, North Carolina*

Copyright © 2006 by Brook Ashley
All rights reserved under
International and Pan-American Copyright Conventions
Printed in Canada.

The paper in this book meets the guidelines for permanence and durability of the Committee on Production Guidelines for Book Longevity of the Council on Library Resources.

The photographs in this book were taken by Dare Wright during several visits to Ocracoke in the 1950s. After writing the accompanying text, she printed and hand-bound this homage to the island into a single cardboard-mounted volume. That original book was restored in 2005. Brook Ashley, as the sole heir to the estate of Dare Wright, is the owner of any and all rights pertaining to all photographs, photographic collections, books, artworks, letters, and other intellectual properties that were created by or otherwise belonged to Dare Wright. Neither this book nor any of its contents may be copied, reproduced, or reprinted in any manner, form, or fashion without the express written consent of Brook Ashley.

Library of Congress Cataloging-in-Publication Data
Wright, Dare.
Ocracoke in the fifties / photographs and narrative by Dare Wright ; edited by Brook Ashley and John Ogilvie.
p. cm.
ISBN-13: 978-0-89587-322-4 (alk. paper)
ISBN-10: 0-89587-322-2
1. Ocracoke Island (N.C.)—Pictorial works. 2. Ocracoke Island (N.C.)—Description and travel. 3. Ocracoke Island (N.C.)—Social life and customs—20th century. I. Ashley, Brook, 1947- II. Ogilvie, John. III. Title
F262.H9W75 2006
551.46'1348—dc22 2006000291

Design by Debra Long Hampton

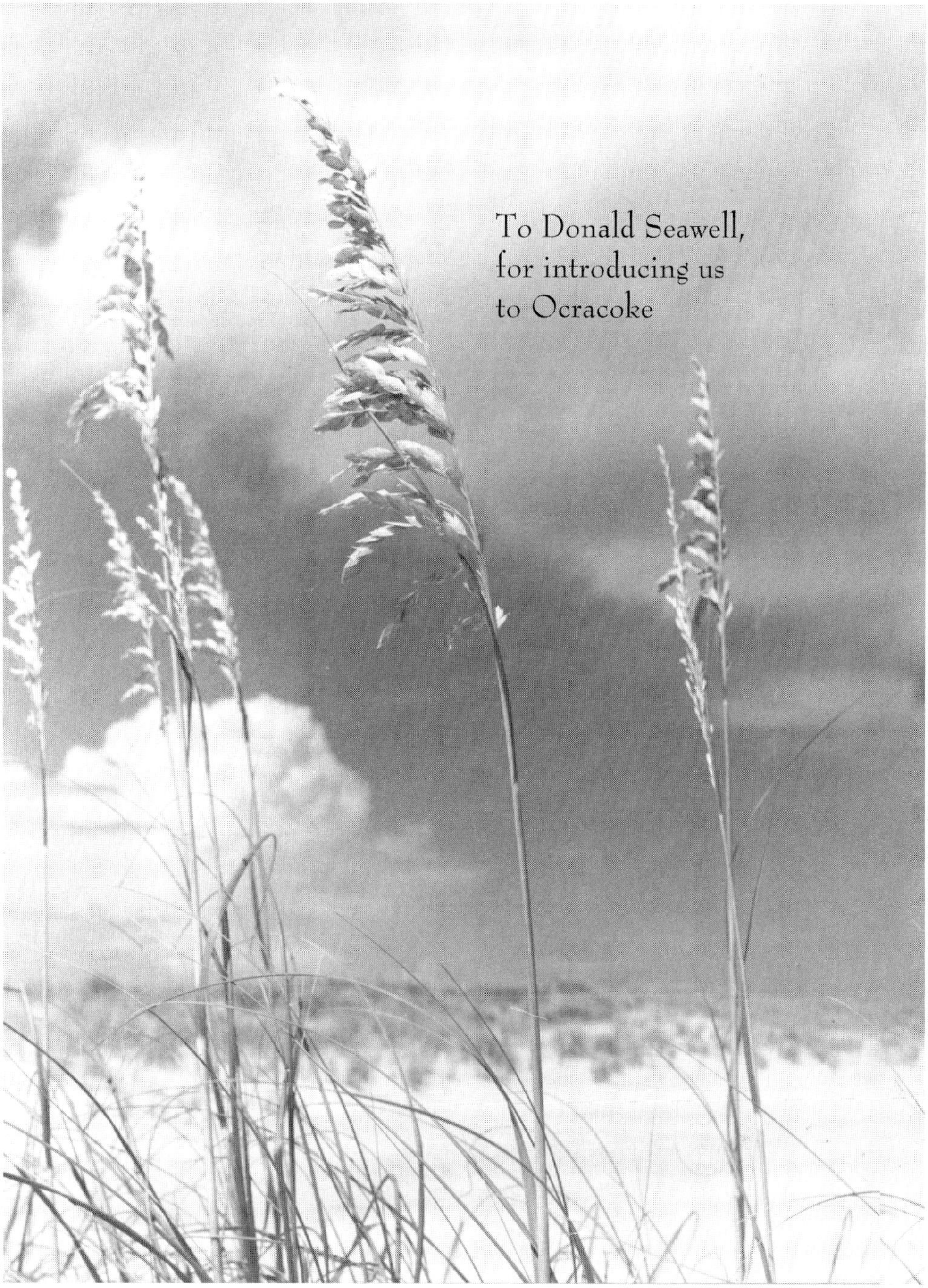

To Donald Seawell,
for introducing us
to Ocracoke

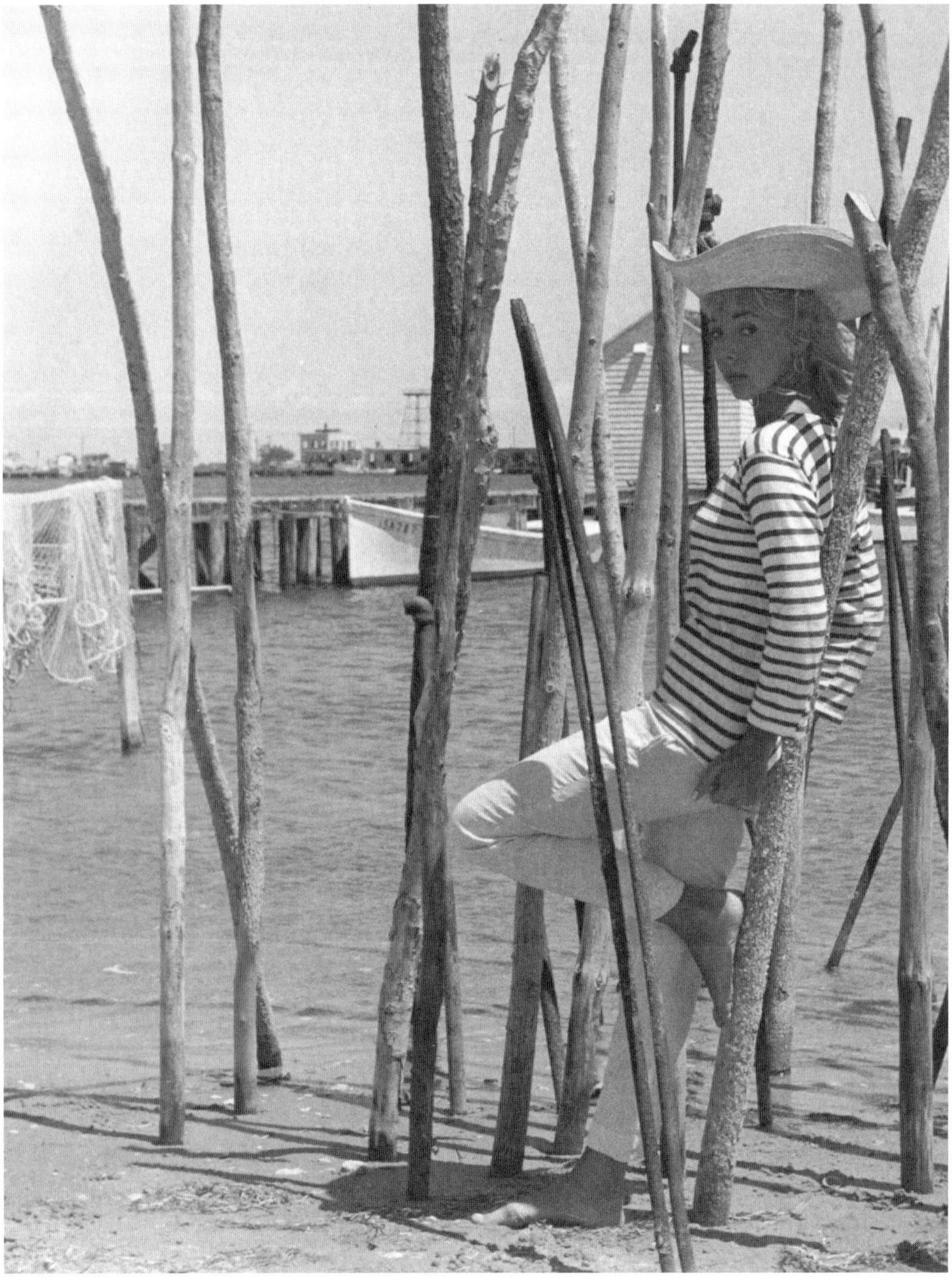

Foreword

Dare Wright (1914-2001) was a model, fashion photographer, and children's author who lived in New York City. Her best-selling children's stories began with *The Lonely Doll* in 1957. This classic book told the story of a lonely doll named Edith and the two bears who came to keep her company. Illustrated with Dare's haunting black-and-white photographs, the book was an immediate success. It was followed in 1958 by *Holiday for Edith & the Bears*, which Dare photographed on Ocracoke Island. Dare wrote eighteen more children's books (one of them unpublished), but she also intended to complete a tribute to Ocracoke Island for the adult market. She left me the hand-bound draft of this unpublished book, along with several boxes of her Ocracoke photographs, when she died. My husband, John Ogilvie, and I have restored the photographs and edited Dare's text to create this volume. Dare's notes suggest several possible titles, but *Ocracoke in the Fifties* seems the most appropriate.

I grew up in Manhattan considering Dare as my second mother. Having no children of her own, she often borrowed me from my parents. Overnights with Dare meant eating flan for dinner and concocting fanciful tales of pirates and buried treasure. There was something almost otherworldly about Dare, and she retained a child's inquisitiveness throughout her life.

There has been an astounding resurgence of interest in Dare and her work. Three of her children's books are back in print, with more to follow. Articles about her have appeared in the *New York Times* and other newspapers around the country. She has been the subject of a biography, several magazine articles, and innumerable Internet blogs. Dare's Web site (www.darewright.com) has received over five thousand visitors in a single month. There will soon be a feature film based on her life.

My father, a native North Carolinian, introduced Dare to Ocracoke Island in the early 1950s. She was immediately captivated by its wild beauty and miles of unpopulated beaches. When Dare began photographing the island and its people, it was already clear to her that she was documenting a vanishing way of life. She revisited Ocracoke many times and waited over a decade after taking these pictures before she wrote the text. More than thirty years have passed since then, and the island has absorbed outside influences unimagined by Dare or the subjects in her photographs.

I remember Dare's Ocracoke from my childhood, when the unshod wild ponies came right up onto my grandmother's porch. My husband first visited the island as a young man, and we both retain memories of an island way of life that no longer exists.

Nostalgic without being sentimental, this book is Dare's homage to an island and a culture poised between the tides of historical tradition and inevitable change.

Brook Ashley
Executor of the estate of Dare Wright

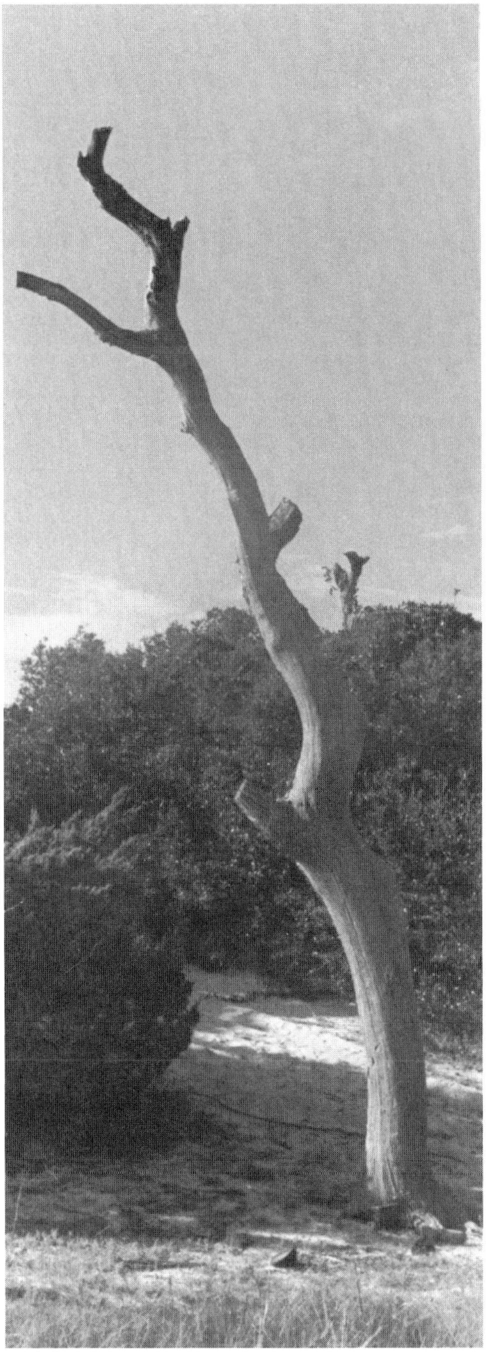

Acknowledgements

The following North Carolinians are owed thanks for their help with this project: Alton Ballance, Philip Howard, and Anne Russell.

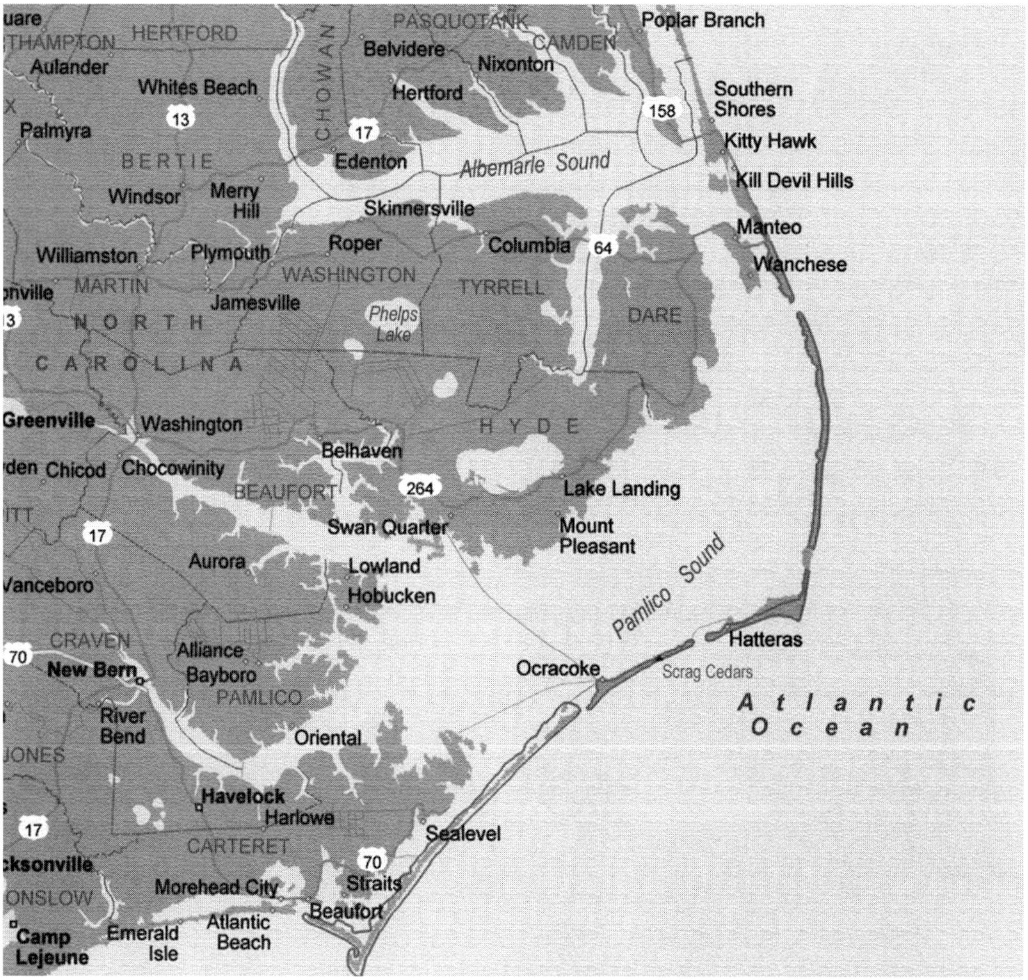
Poplar Branch
HERTFORD
PASQUOTANK
CAMDEN
Aulander
Belvidere
Nixonton
CHOWAN
Whites Beach
Hertford
Southern Shores
158
13
17
Palmyra
Kitty Hawk
Edenton
Albemarle Sound
BERTIE
Kill Devil Hills
Windsor
Merry Hill
Skinnersville
Manteo
Williamston
Plymouth
Roper
Columbia
64
Wanchese
MARTIN
WASHINGTON
TYRRELL
Jamesville
Phelps Lake
DARE
NORTH
CAROLINA
Greenville
Washington
HYDE
Belhaven
Chicod
Chocowinity
Lake Landing
BEAUFORT
264
Swan Quarter
Mount Pleasant
17
Aurora
Lowland
Pamlico Sound
Vanceboro
Hobucken
CRAVEN
Hatteras
70
Alliance
New Bern
Bayboro
Ocracoke
Scrag Cedars
PAMLICO
Atlantic Ocean
River Bend
Oriental
JONES
Havelock
Harlowe
17
Sealevel
CARTERET
70
Straits
ONSLOW
Morehead City
Beaufort
Camp Lejeune
Emerald Isle
Atlantic Beach

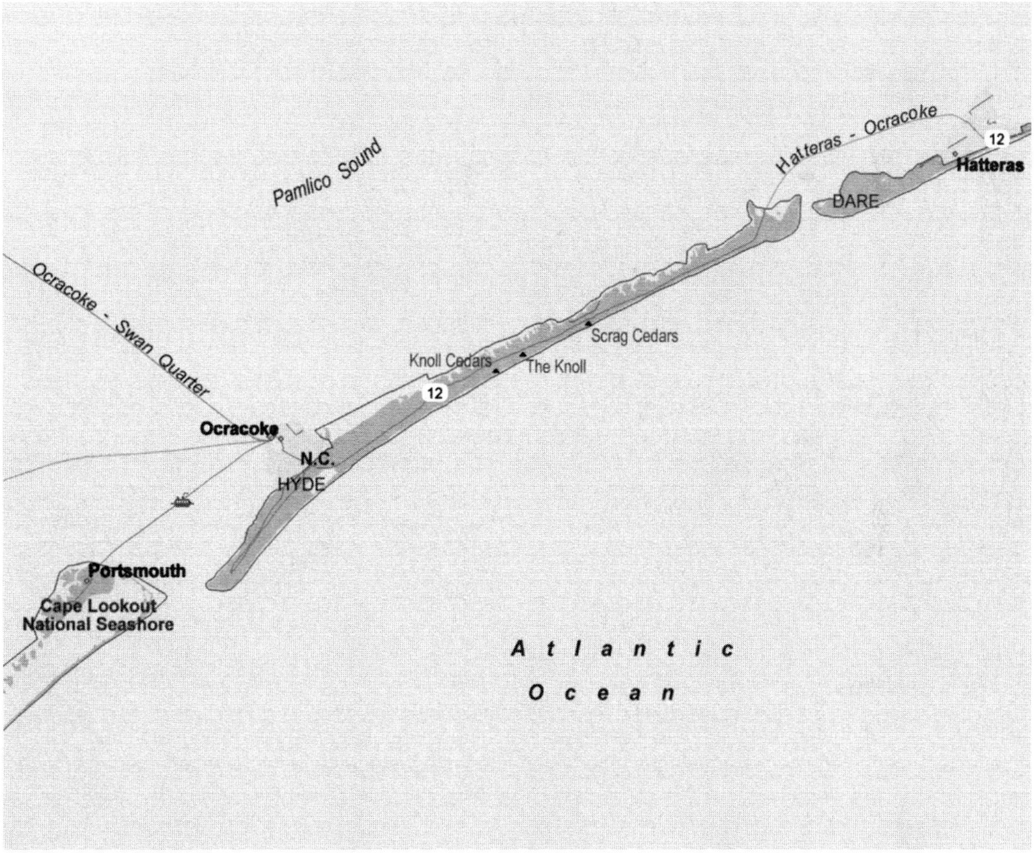
Pamlico Sound
Hatteras - Ocracoke
12
Hatteras
DARE
Ocracoke - Swan Quarter
Scrag Cedars
Knoll Cedars
The Knoll
12
Ocracoke
N.C.
HYDE
Portsmouth
Cape Lookout
National Seashore
Atlantic
Ocean

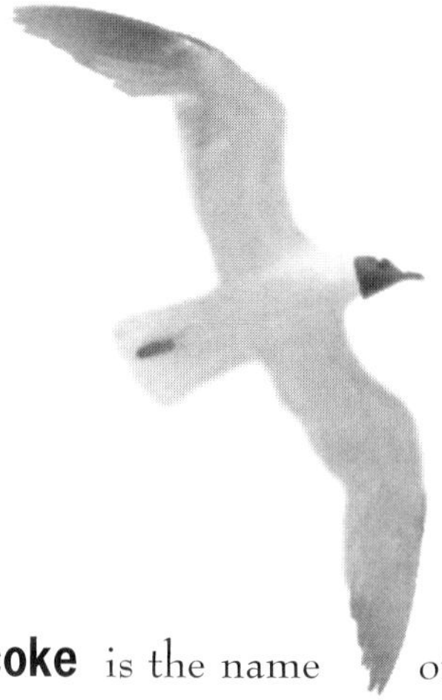

Ocracoke is the name of an island. It is a name that lingers in the mind, and an island that lingers in the heart. It is a place of sea and sky, of drifting sand and crying gulls, a slim sand bar in the Atlantic where centuries of isolation have created a special quality of life. It is part of the barrier reefs of North Carolina known as the Outer Banks, and its history is woven into the beginning of America.

It was on Ocracoke in 1585 that Sir Walter Raleigh's expedition first stepped ashore. The same expedition established the earliest European colony in America on nearby Roanoke Island.

Yet earlier than that, French and Spanish exploring parties had landed on the Outer Banks. Those adventurers thought they were standing on an isthmus looking west at another ocean, beyond which lay China and the wonders of the Orient. What they were really seeing was the shallow, thirty-mile-wide Pamlico Sound, beyond which lay the coast of North Carolina and the unexplored American continent.

As settlements grew numerous on the shores of the mainland, the Outer Banks were a welcome protection from Atlantic storms and invasion. But they were also a nuisance because their waters were too shallow for the trade brought by deep-draft oceangoing ships. The only entrances to the sound were the narrow and constantly changing inlets between the islands.

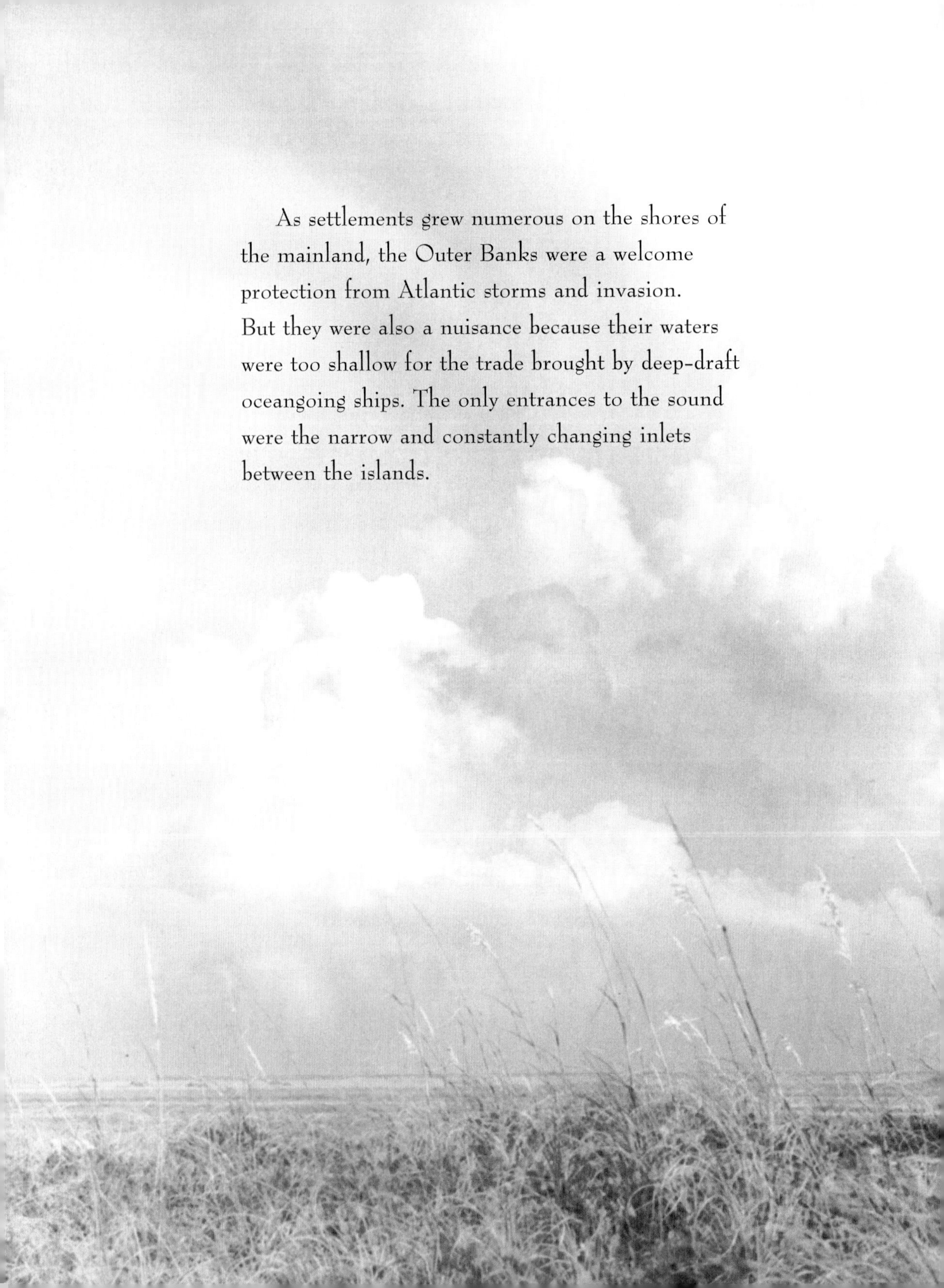

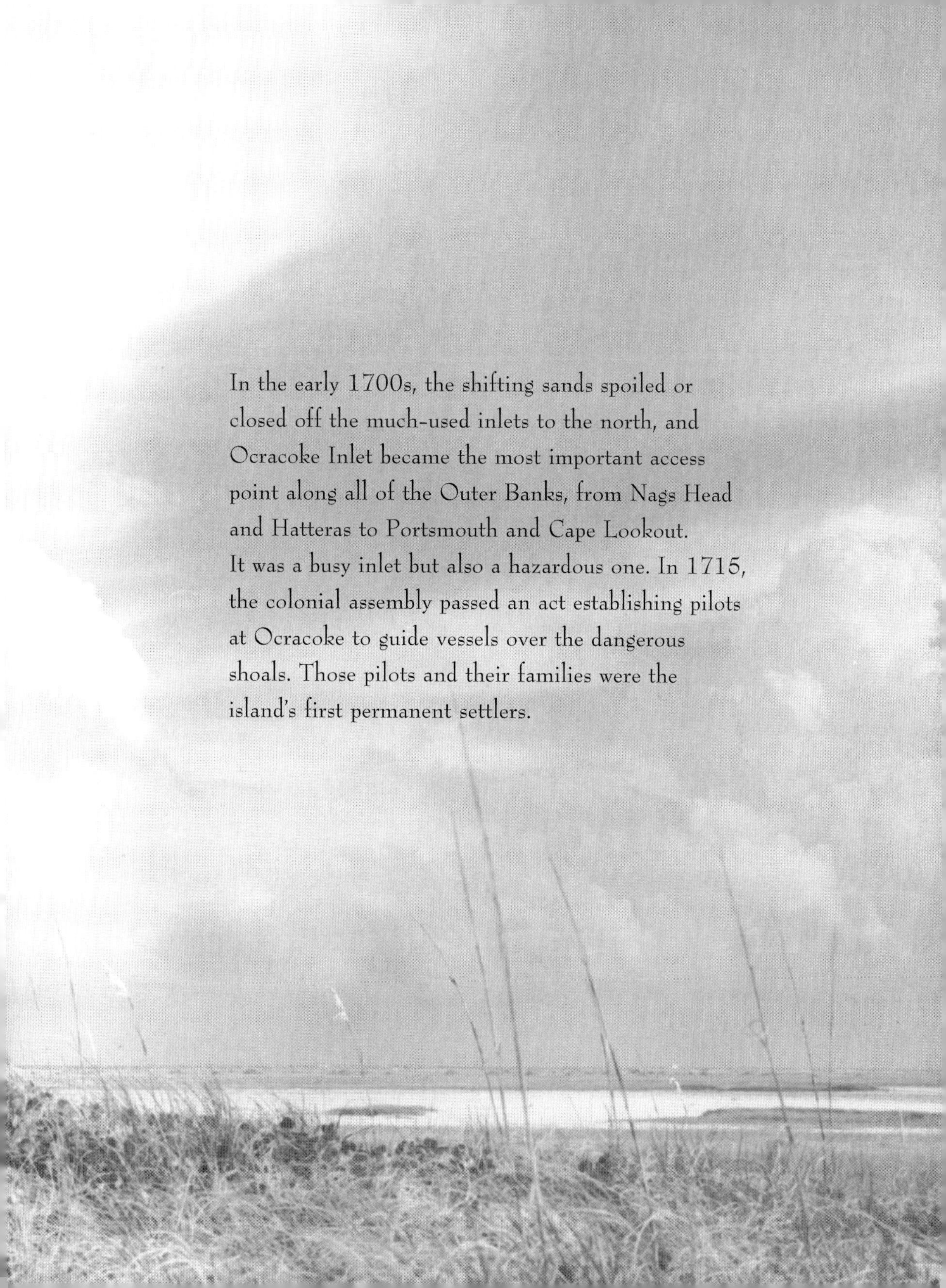

In the early 1700s, the shifting sands spoiled or closed off the much-used inlets to the north, and Ocracoke Inlet became the most important access point along all of the Outer Banks, from Nags Head and Hatteras to Portsmouth and Cape Lookout. It was a busy inlet but also a hazardous one. In 1715, the colonial assembly passed an act establishing pilots at Ocracoke to guide vessels over the dangerous shoals. Those pilots and their families were the island's first permanent settlers.

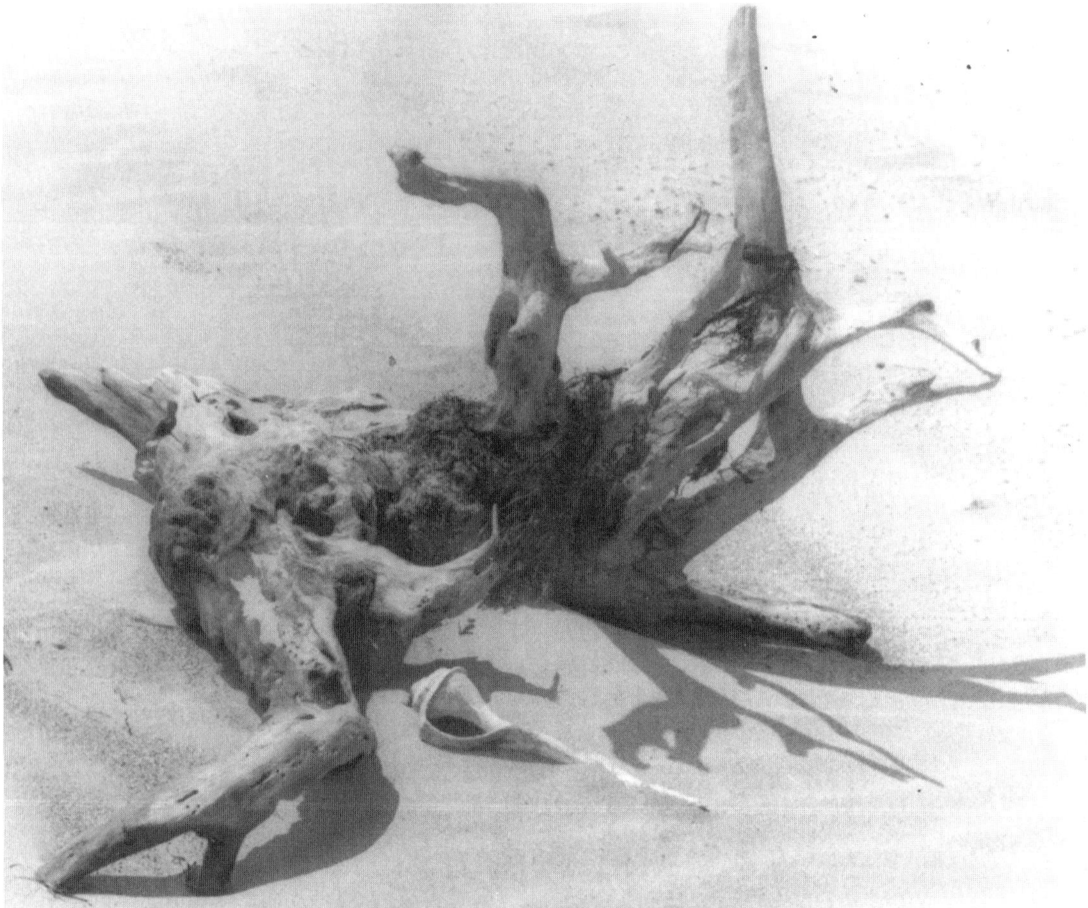

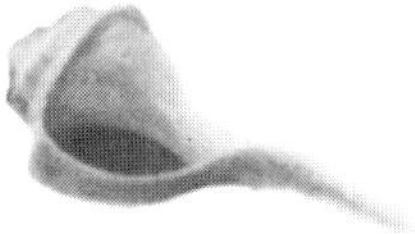

Nature wasn't Ocracoke's only enemy. For a brief wild period, pirates preyed successfully upon shipping along the length of the coast. The notorious Blackbeard himself established a base on the island. And in the 1740s, the Spanish boldly camped on Ocracoke while they raided merchant traffic.

More violence came with the American Revolution. The British blockaded the eastern seaboard's great ports but at first did not think Ocracoke important enough to bother about. "The contemptible port of Ocracoke," a Royal governor called it. When they finally realized how many supplies reached the American army through narrow Ocracoke Inlet, the British found there wasn't a great deal they could do about it. The weather and the ever-changing shoals kept their large warships at bay. Ocracoke's pilots were on the patriots' side, and small American vessels slipped through under the noses of the British. Desperately needed provisions for Washington's troops starving in the snow of Valley Forge came through Ocracoke Inlet.

In the peace after the Revolutionary War was won, both Ocracoke and its neighboring town of Portsmouth across the inlet grew and prospered. Where today Ocracoke's sandy southern tip slides away into an empty channel, you once would have seen sails by the hundreds—brigs, sloops, and schooners loading, unloading, and waiting for the wind. The port teemed with shipping. In 1794, the first lighthouse was authorized.

British warships again appeared off the Banks during the War of 1812. English troops actually landed briefly on Ocracoke. American privateers operated from its shelter.

Ocracoke might have remained a great port if nature had not taken a hand in things. Shifting currents began to fill in the channel, and dredging did not help. In 1846, a violent hurricane swept the Banks, cutting two new inlets through the heart of Hatteras Island. By the beginning of the Civil War, Hatteras Inlet had attracted nearly all of Ocracoke's trade, leaving Ocracoke outside the current of history.

With the income from piloting gone, the island's people turned to a quiet life of fishing and shrimping. Outsiders were few. They came for the marvelous fishing and hunting, or just for the marvelous peace.

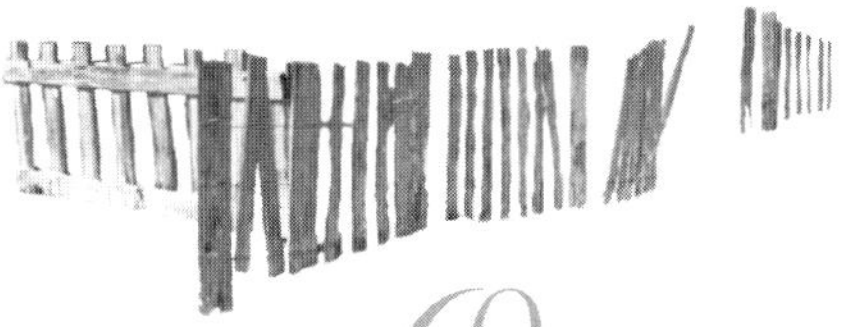

Ocracoke remains a slow-paced island. Its fifteen narrow miles of sand flats and shifting dunes seem pinned to the earth by its lighthouse. The frame houses of the town cluster around an almost land-locked harbor on the southwest corner of the island, on Pamlico Sound. The houses seem loosely scattered along roadways of deep sand.

Peaceful, yes, but this is also a place of storms. Located in the path of hurricanes, it is always at the mercy of the elements. Ocean tides rip through the inlet. Wind-driven waves wash over the island, invading houses, making new inlets, rearranging the beaches. Nature has changed Ocracoke many times through the years but never destroyed it. Today, it is man who is changing the island. Ocracoke is no longer inaccessible, and like so many things in our accelerating culture, the island has changed more in the last 10 years than in the previous 250. It wasn't

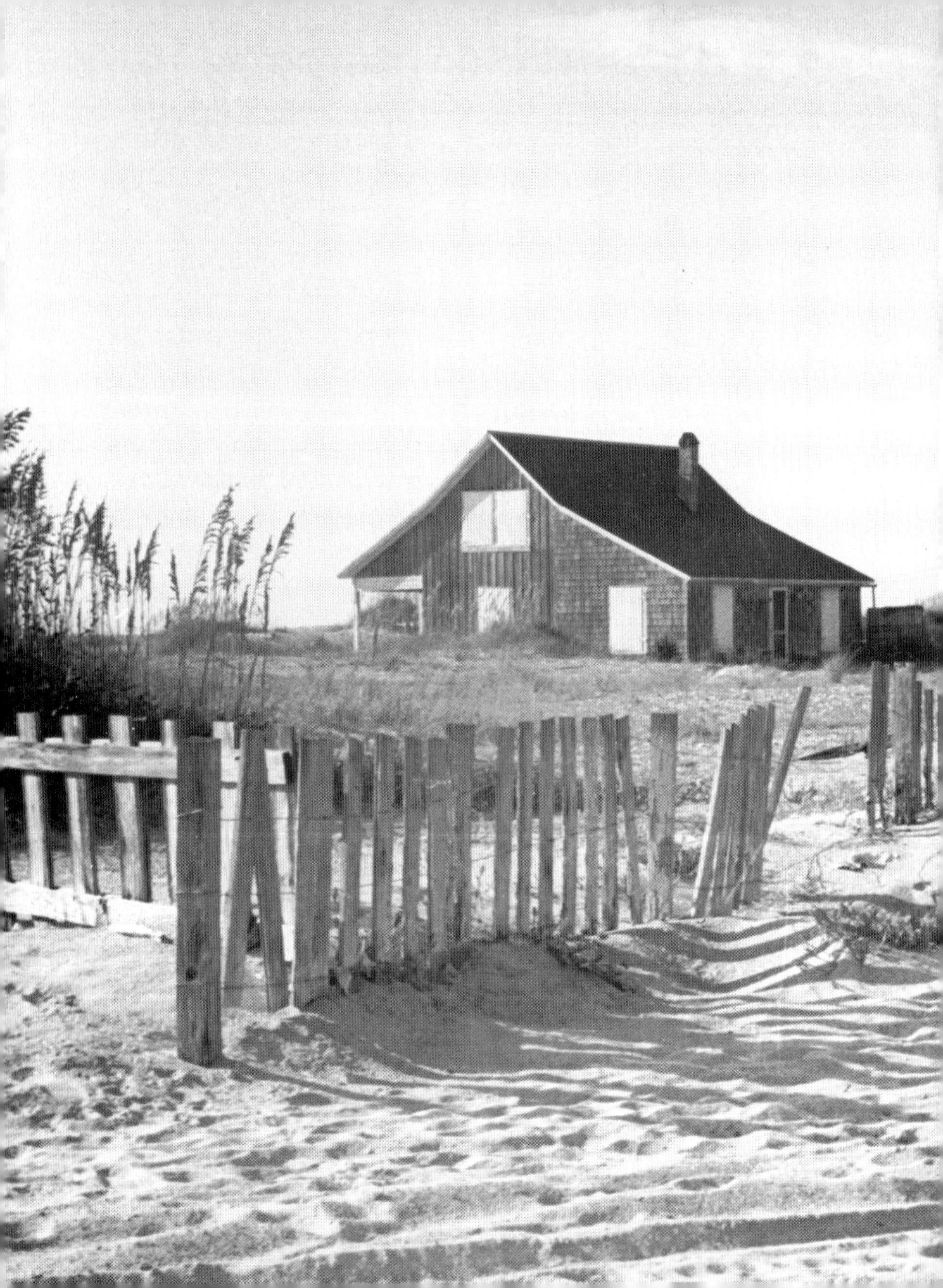

so long ago that Ocracoke had no jail, no policeman, no doctor, no bank, no funeral parlor, no supermarket, no billboards, no local government, no local taxes, no television, and no surfaced road. Its only telephone, when it worked, belonged to the Coast Guard. If someone called for you, an obliging Coast Guardsman jumped into a Jeep to find you.

The island does happily without a great many modern devices, but telephones are now common. Television seems not to have swamped the town's humanity. The most important change is a surfaced road running the length of the island, with ferry service at both ends. This means a stream of tourists passing through, accompanied by the motels, stores, and restaurants necessary to serve them. The road has brought a new prosperity for the islanders, and new conveniences. But what a pity if progress transforms Ocracoke's uniqueness into the commercial homogeneity overtaking the rest of the world.

Thankfully, except for the town and the area immediately around it, the island is now protected. It has become a part of Cape Hatteras National Seashore, America's first National Seashore. The Park Service is fighting the wind and the water by building a sea wall of dunes and placing beach grass to hold the sand in place. It is trying to preserve the island's wildness for the birds, the fish, and the people of America to whom it now belongs. Look, then, at these photographs of the island of Ocracoke—partly as it is, partly as it was, entirely as it appeared to me.

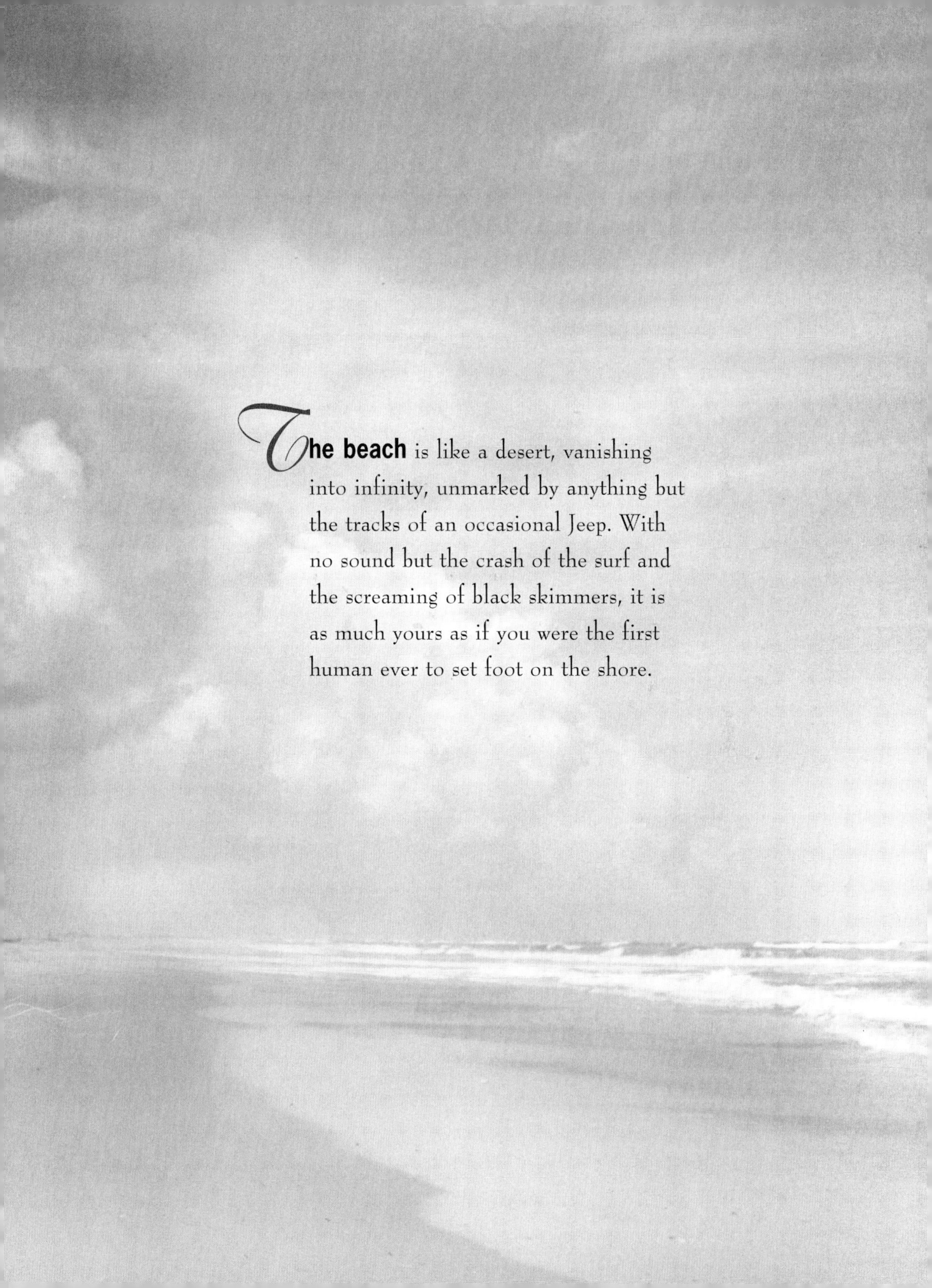

The beach is like a desert, vanishing into infinity, unmarked by anything but the tracks of an occasional Jeep. With no sound but the crash of the surf and the screaming of black skimmers, it is as much yours as if you were the first human ever to set foot on the shore.

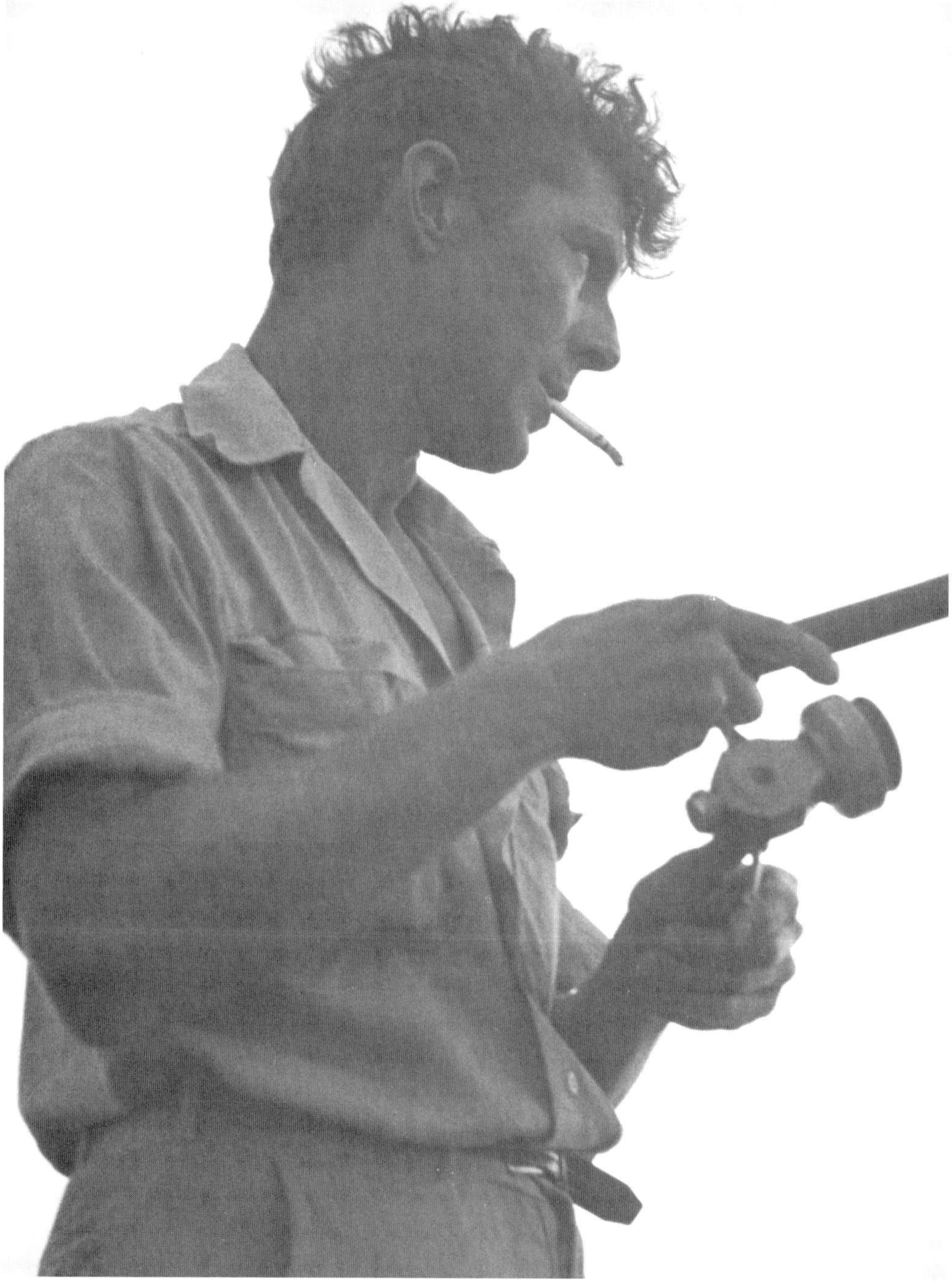

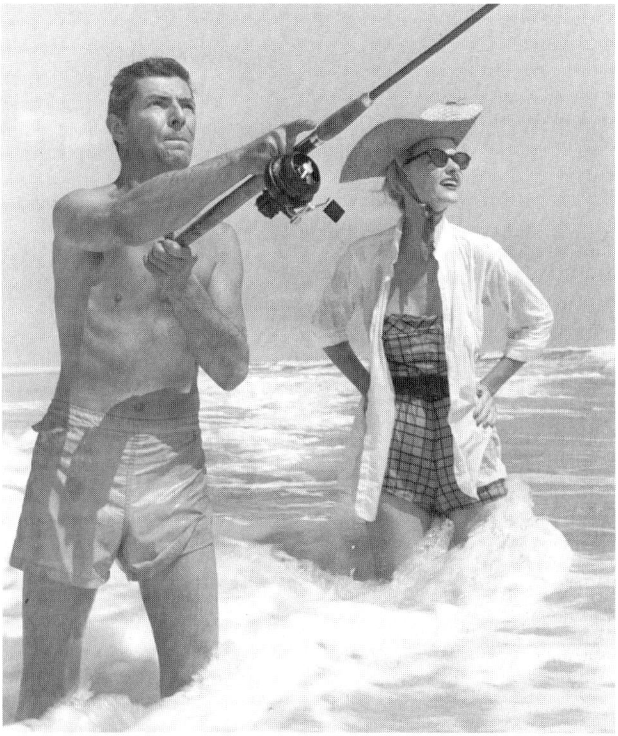

Sometimes, you'll see a fisherman casting in the surf. The Gulf Stream is only twelve miles offshore, and a wonderful variety of fish come out of these waters. In the spring and fall, the drum, or channel bass, run fifty, sixty, or even seventy pounds.

Or a child fascinated by the twinkling feet of the shorebirds as they follow the waves in and out to feed on the tiny periwinkles, which appear by the hundreds as each wave recedes, then frantically dig to bury themselves safely beneath the sand.

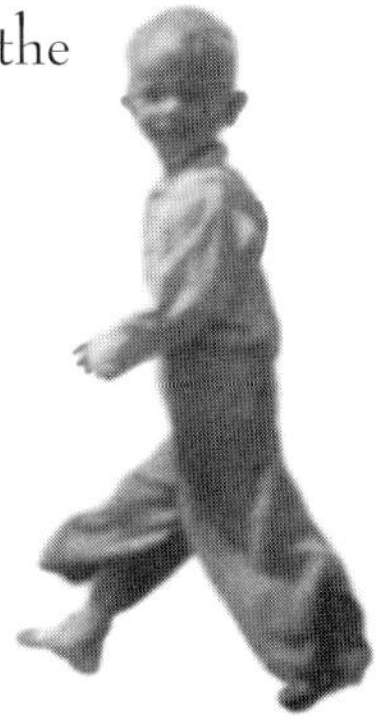

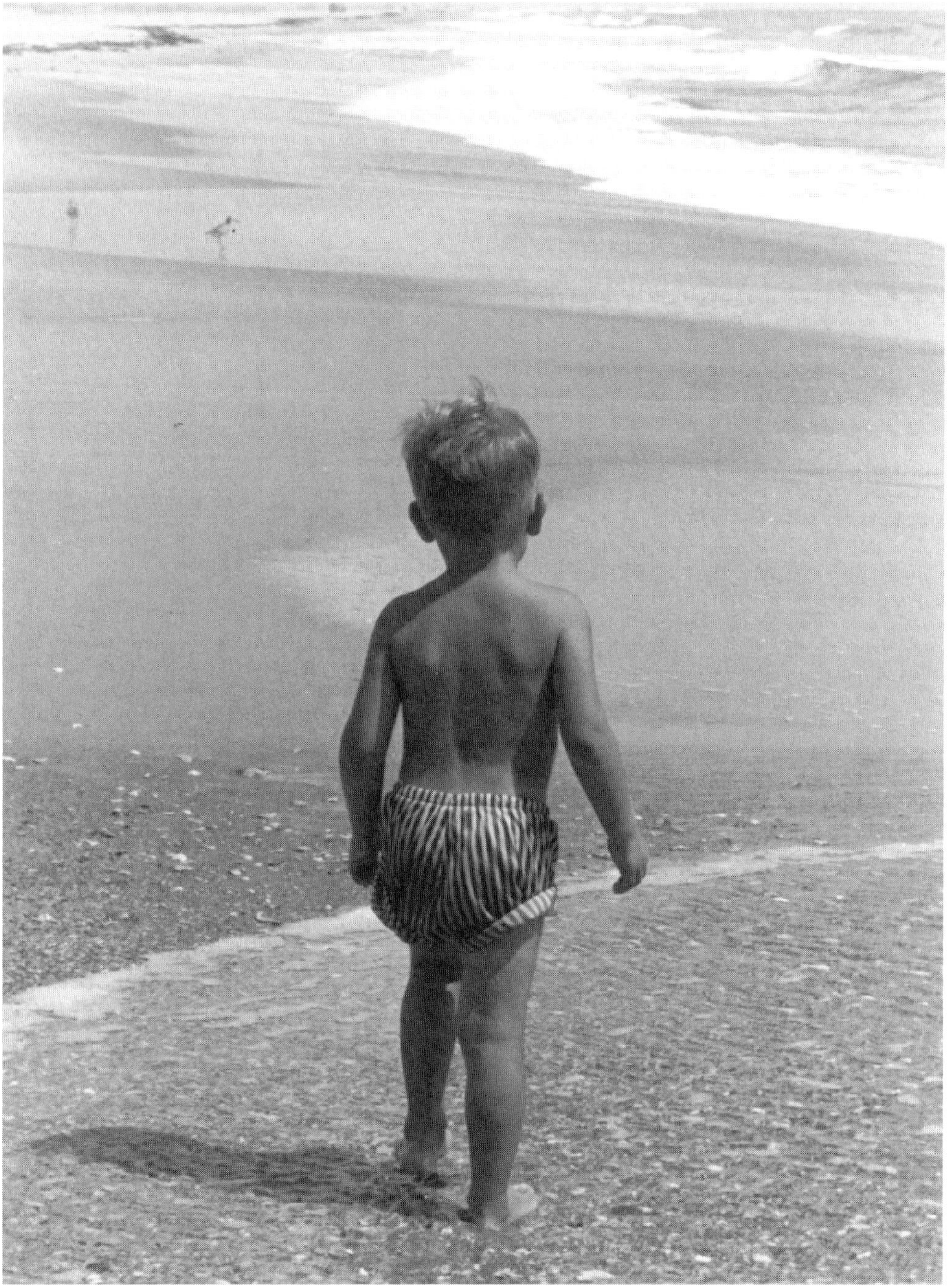

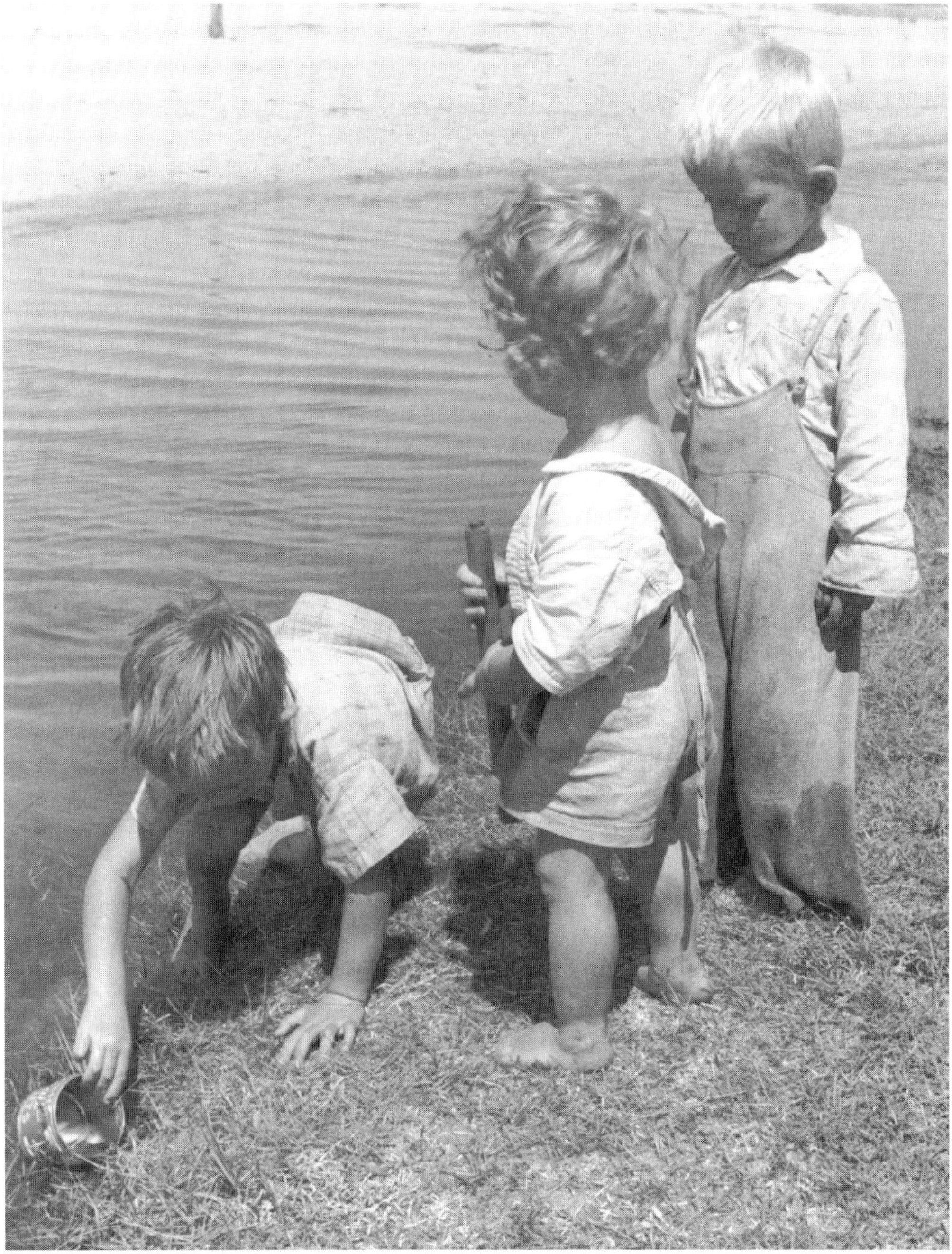

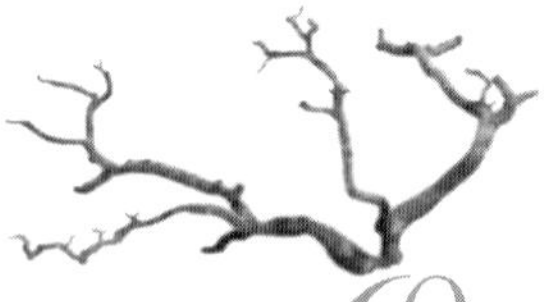

Or there might be a swimmer in the swirling breakers. The waters are dangerous not for their roughness but because of the sand bars, rip currents, and undertow.

The sea makes daily offerings to the beach. You'll find driftwood polished into fantasies by wind and water, and shells ground down to their exquisite skeletons. In a day, these sea offerings can vanish. The wind and sand can build anything, large or small, into a dune, beautiful when constructed with nature's throwaways, ugly when crafted from man's.

Year after year, the dunes form anew and march inland. They have swallowed whole forests of live oak, cedar, pine, and grapevine that clothed the island when white men first saw it. Men cut the trees for lumber and let their livestock graze on the grasses and brush. The sand was freed for the wind to seize. The wind gathered and piled it against anything that stood in its way, and slowly the dunes smothered what man had left of the forests. And still the dunes move, driven by relentless winds. These waves of sand may someday meet the mainland before they end their march.

The bones of countless ships lie beneath these dunes, this seemingly peaceful coast one of the most treacherous on earth. This "Graveyard of the Atlantic" lies just below Cape Hatteras. Here, at Ocracoke, the Gulf Stream and the Labrador Current meet in a confusion of shoals and churning currents.

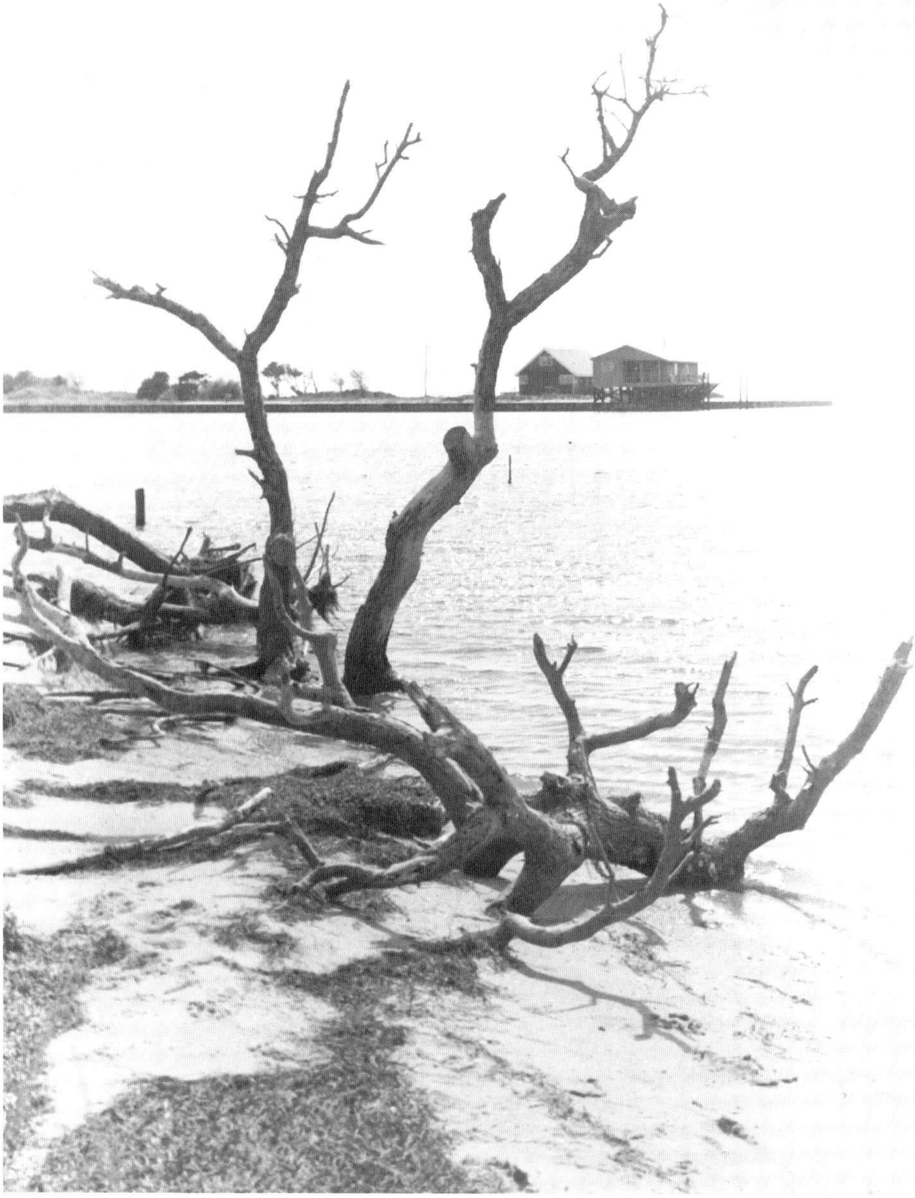

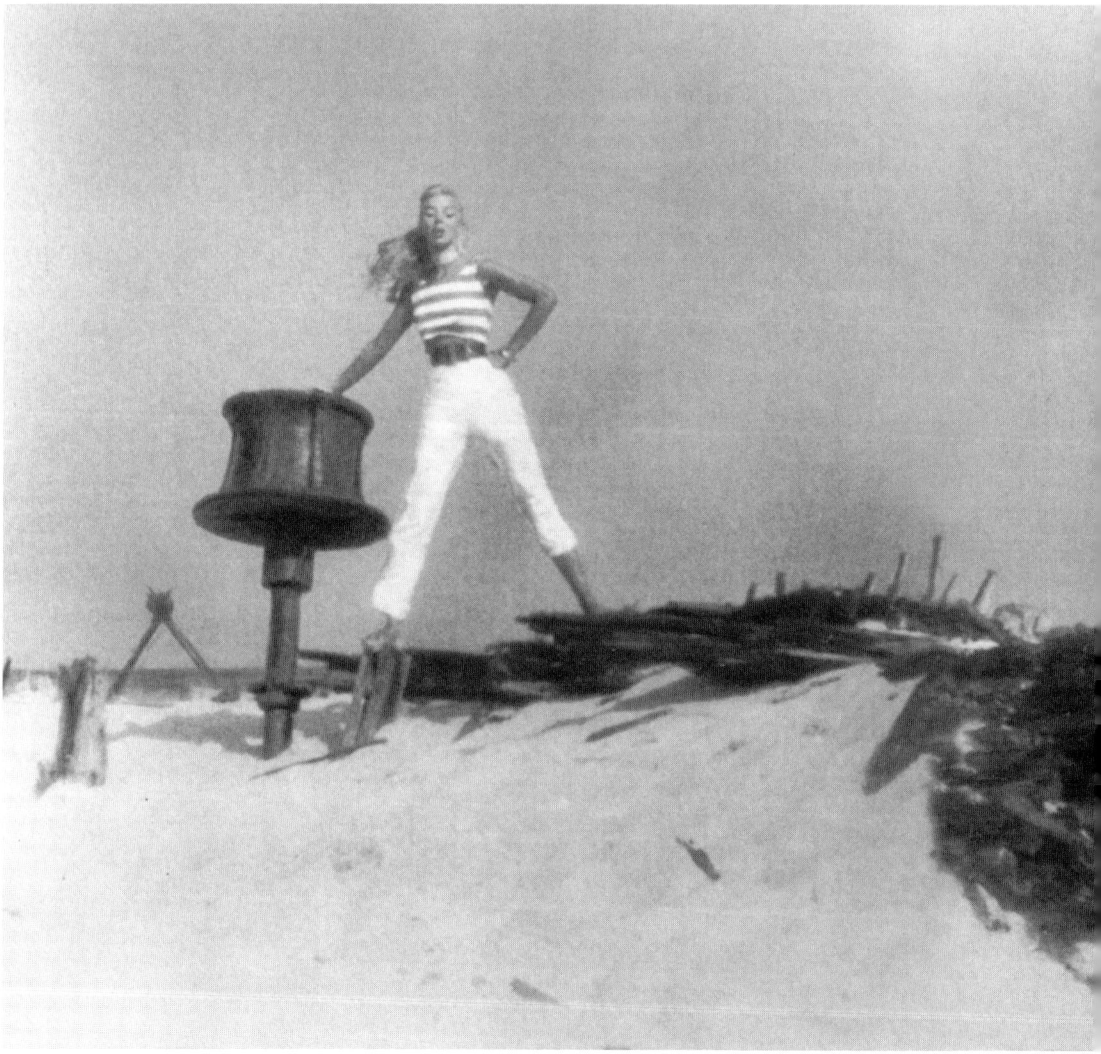

No one knows how many ships lie beneath the sands. The ribs and ancient timbers revealed one year may lie buried the next.

My friends remember the grounded hulls of sailing vessels with decks still intact, sturdy enough for dancing in the moonlight.

Every year, the remnants grow fewer. Some are buried beneath

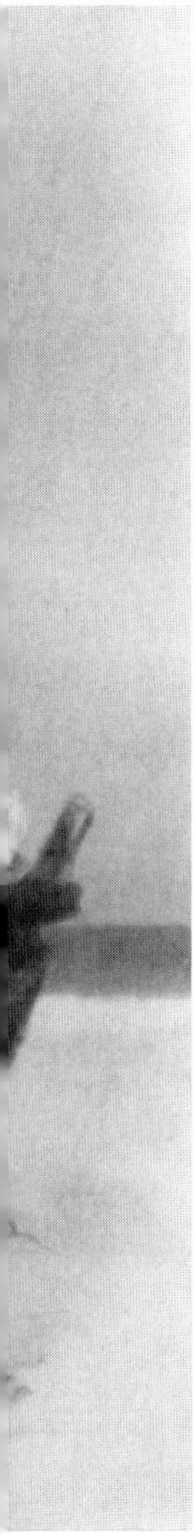

young dunes built by the Park Service. Tourists carry away bits and pieces. But as the physical reminders are lost, the legends persist—like that of the *Carol A. Deering*, a five-masted schooner out of Boston. She ran aground off Hatteras in 1921. Everything was in order on board—the table set for a meal, no sign of the violence to come. There was not a soul on board save a meowing cat. Her hull came ashore on Ocracoke, but her mystery was never solved.

In 1837, there was the *Home*, an elegant new paddle-wheel steamer wrecked with the loss of ninety lives. Twenty-one people drowned on the *Ariosto* in 1899. The six-masted schooner *George W. Wells* was lost in 1913. There have been forty recorded wrecks off the shores of Ocracoke, and who knows how many may have gone unrecorded? It must have been a wild sight to witness the breaking up of a ship in the surf while the men of the Lifesaving Service struggled in the pounding breakers to save crew and passengers. Because of their courage, the loss of life was less than one might expect.

In the early days, if the remains of a ship came ashore, they were quickly stripped. Salvage was sold at auction.

It was not the sea that was the hazard in 1942 when packs of German U-boats lurked off the Outer Banks. The submarines sank so many tankers and other ships that the waters grew to be called "Torpedo Junction." Spilled fuel from the tankers still washes in to stain the beaches.

Thanks to radio and radar, the modern sailor needn't fear the Banks as his ancestors did, but he would still do well to respect this tricky, stormy coast.

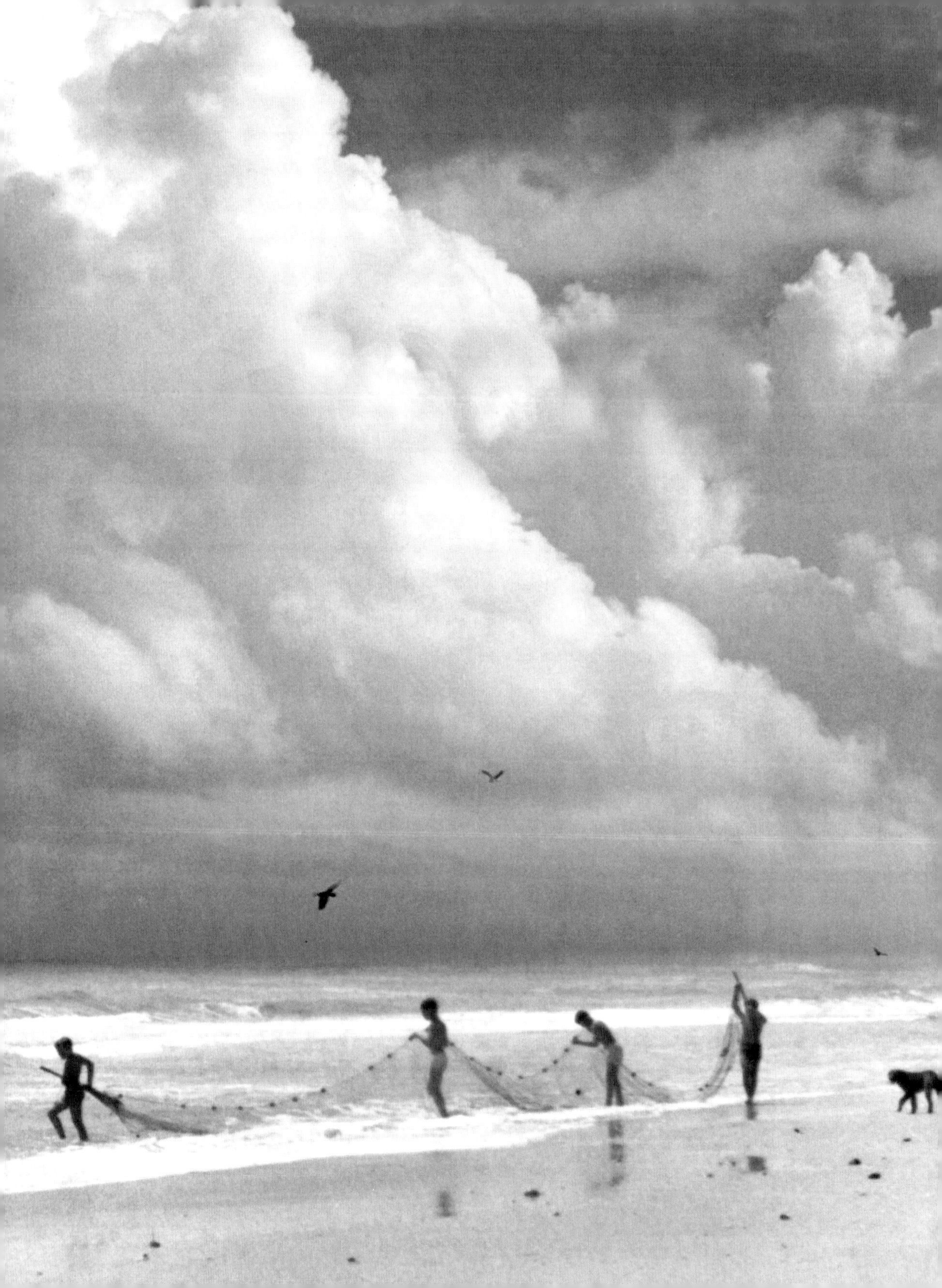

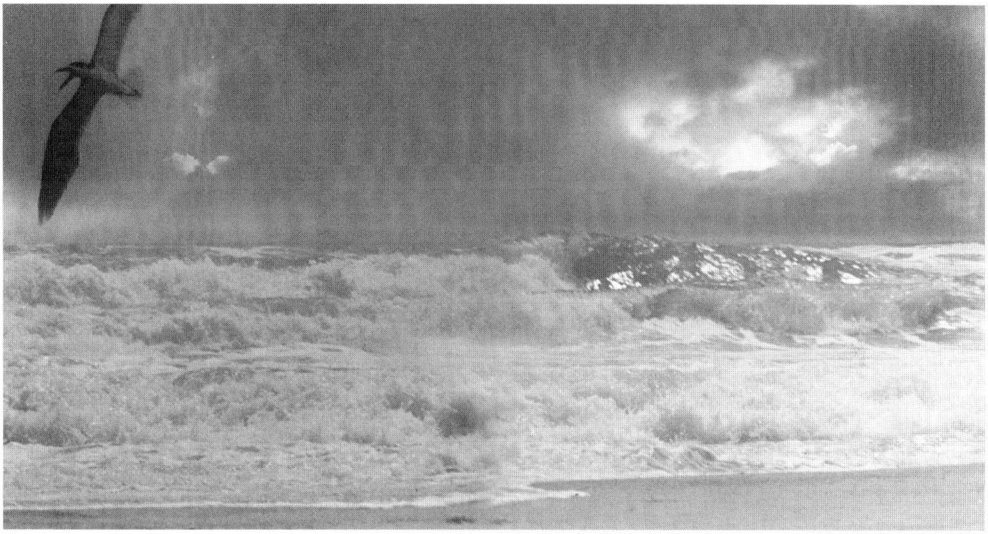

Progress has made no change in the storms that batter Ocracoke. In a minute, the wind can shift, the clouds gather, the world turn dark. The ocean acquires a feeling of great weight.

Sometimes, the water will follow slowly and inexorably at your heels as you cross the mile-wide beach, the flying sand stinging bare legs.

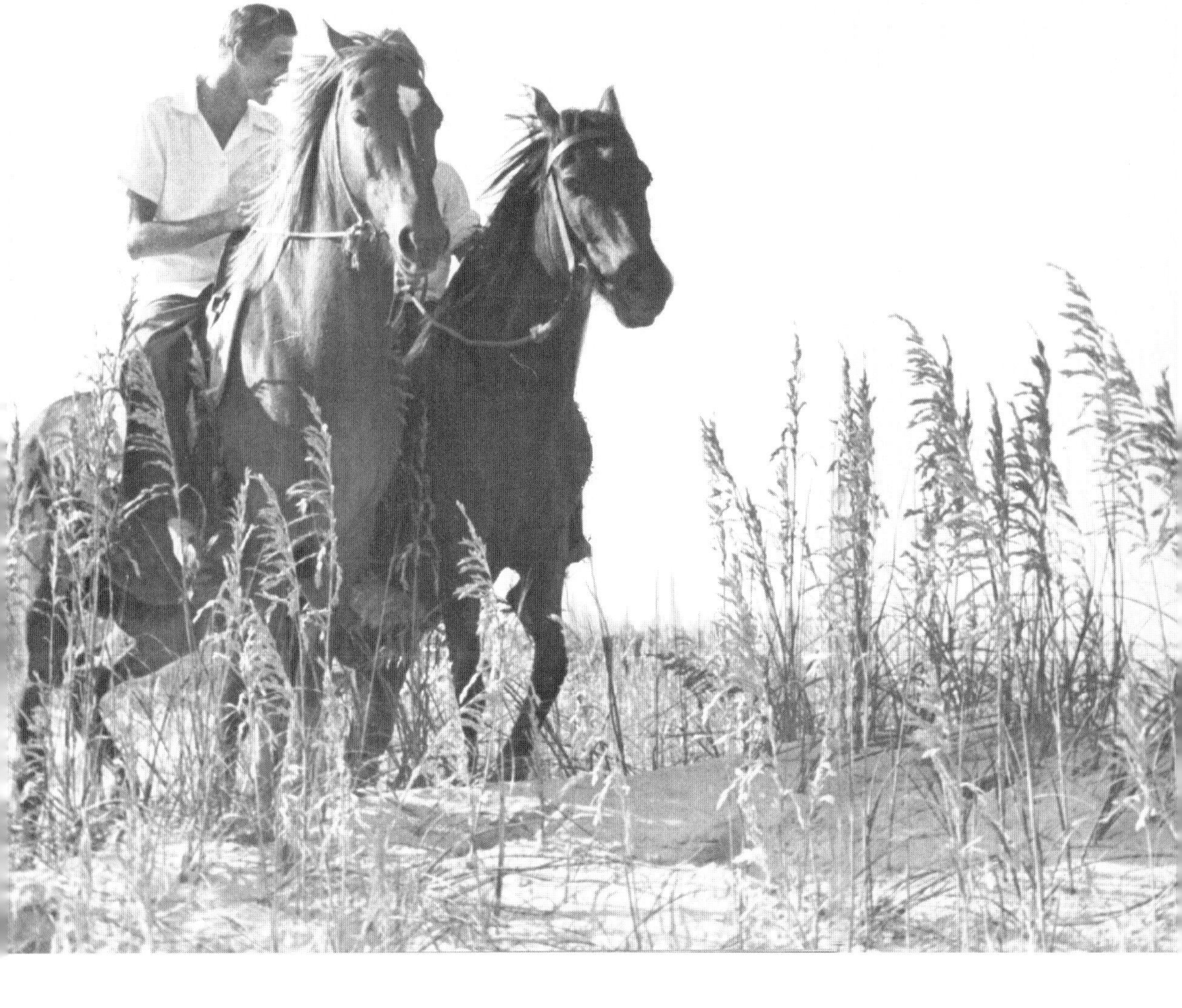

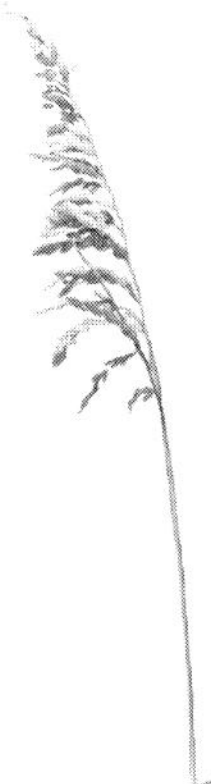

A **storm** can last for days or be gone in an hour. The sun shines again, and the golden sea oats move gently against the sky.

The wild ponies of Ocracoke, undismayed by sudden storms, go back to cropping the harsh grass. Since their Arab ancestors were shipwrecked here a hundred years ago or more, the band has grown tough and hardy, accustomed to wild weather.

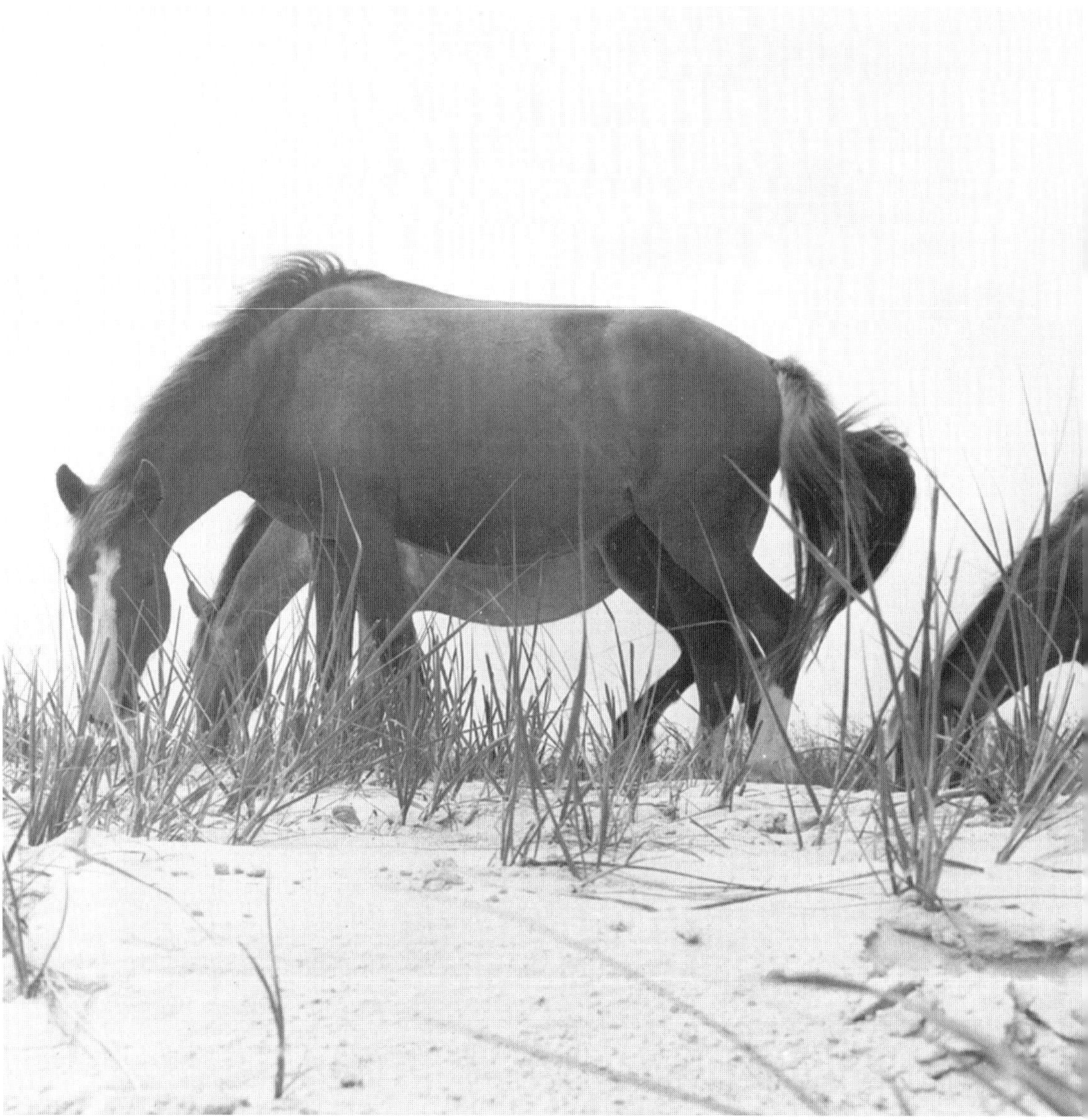

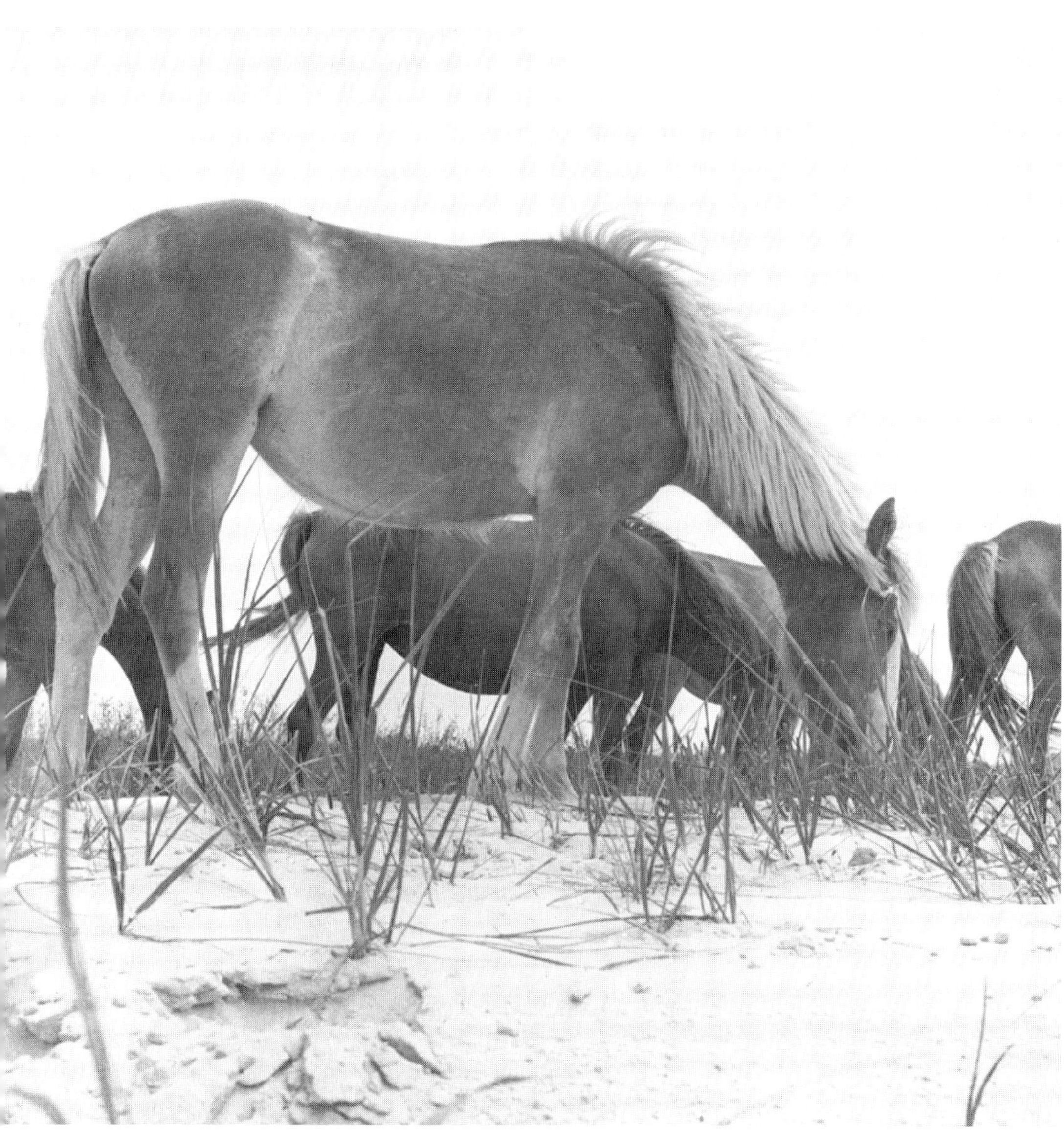

They graze against the skyline, making brown and beige patterns, their long tails swishing and their uncut manes lifting in the wind.

Larger than ponies, smaller than horses, they are wiry and quick. They live on marsh grass and coarse vegetation that would seem a starvation diet for most horses.

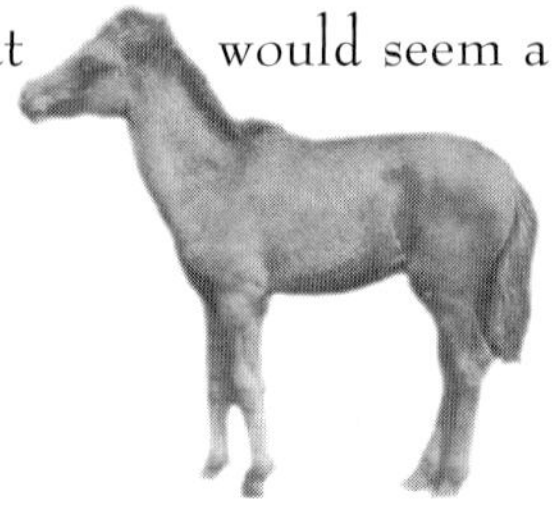

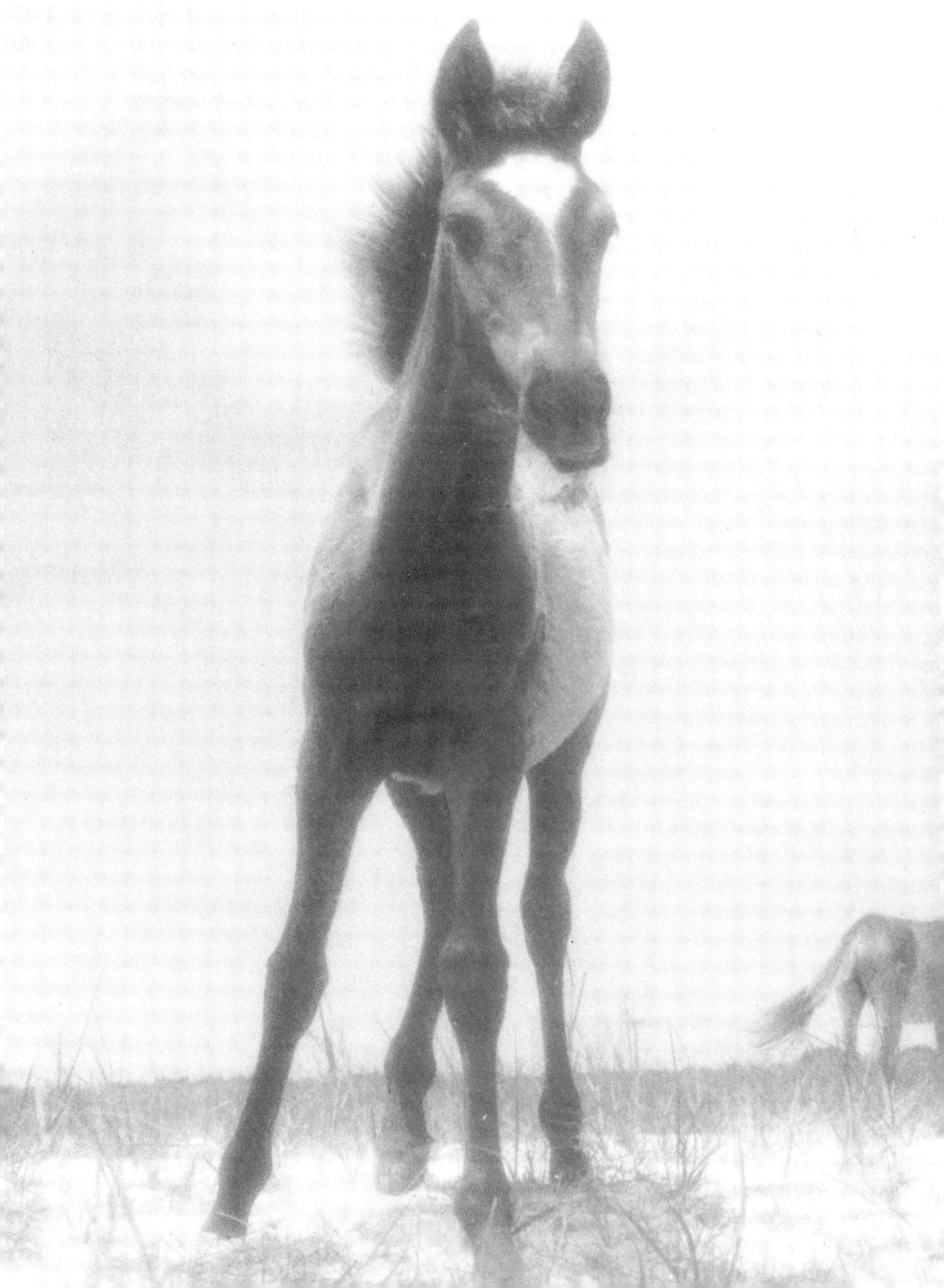

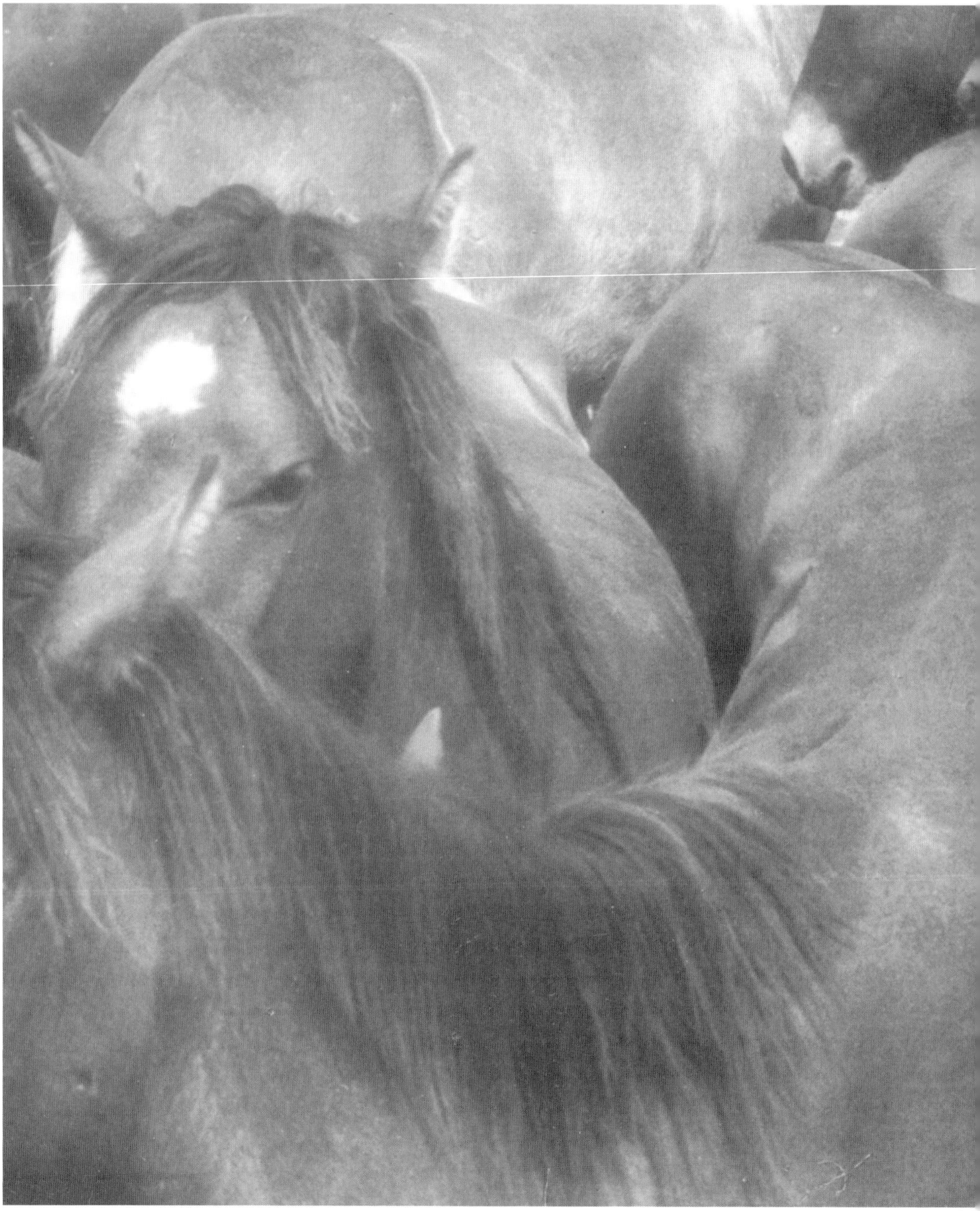

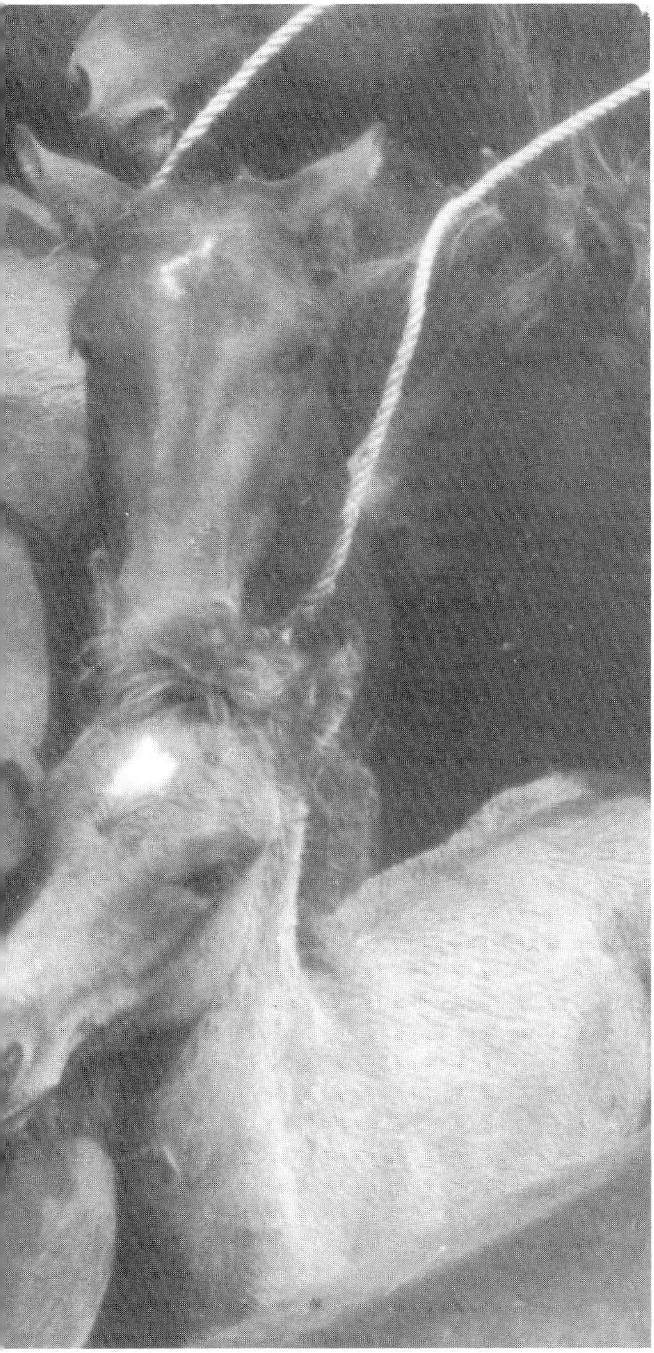

Attempts were made to improve the breed. But the imported stallions were not tough enough to survive the exposure and meager diet. Fresh drinking water, too, was not easy to find.

The native ponies developed their own system of survival. Together, they formed a circle, then pawed a hole in the sand. Dig deep enough and fresh water appeared. Those who didn't dig didn't drink.

The ponies long roamed freely, unshod. So did the island boys who rode them. So could visitors, if they wanted. Ocracoke was a barefoot island.

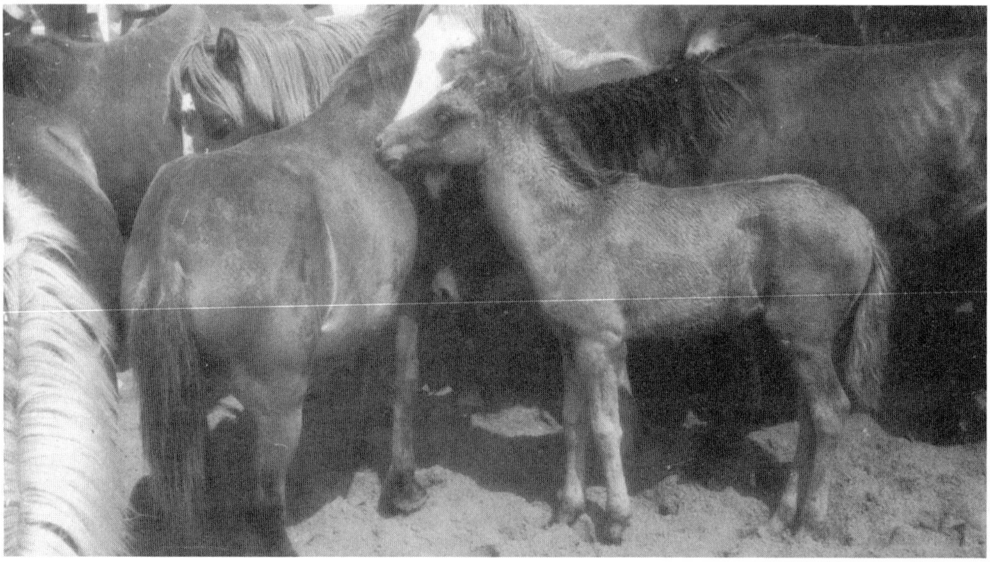

Every Fourth of July in years past, these eastern islanders became cowboys for the "pony penning." Riders started at the northeastern tip of the island and swept the wild band of horses before them. You could have stood atop a dune to watch them race by, charging through tide pools, spray flying behind.

Some of the horses tried to make their escape from the roundup by wading as far as a half-mile into the shallow Pamlico Sound. But in the end, they were all collected, the herd pounding down the sandy village streets and into a corral on the harbor shoreline.

All of the town was there, and visitors from the mainland, too. Some came to buy ponies, some for the excitement of a seashore roundup by a bunch of barefoot cowboys.

The branding of the foals came next. A rope was flung

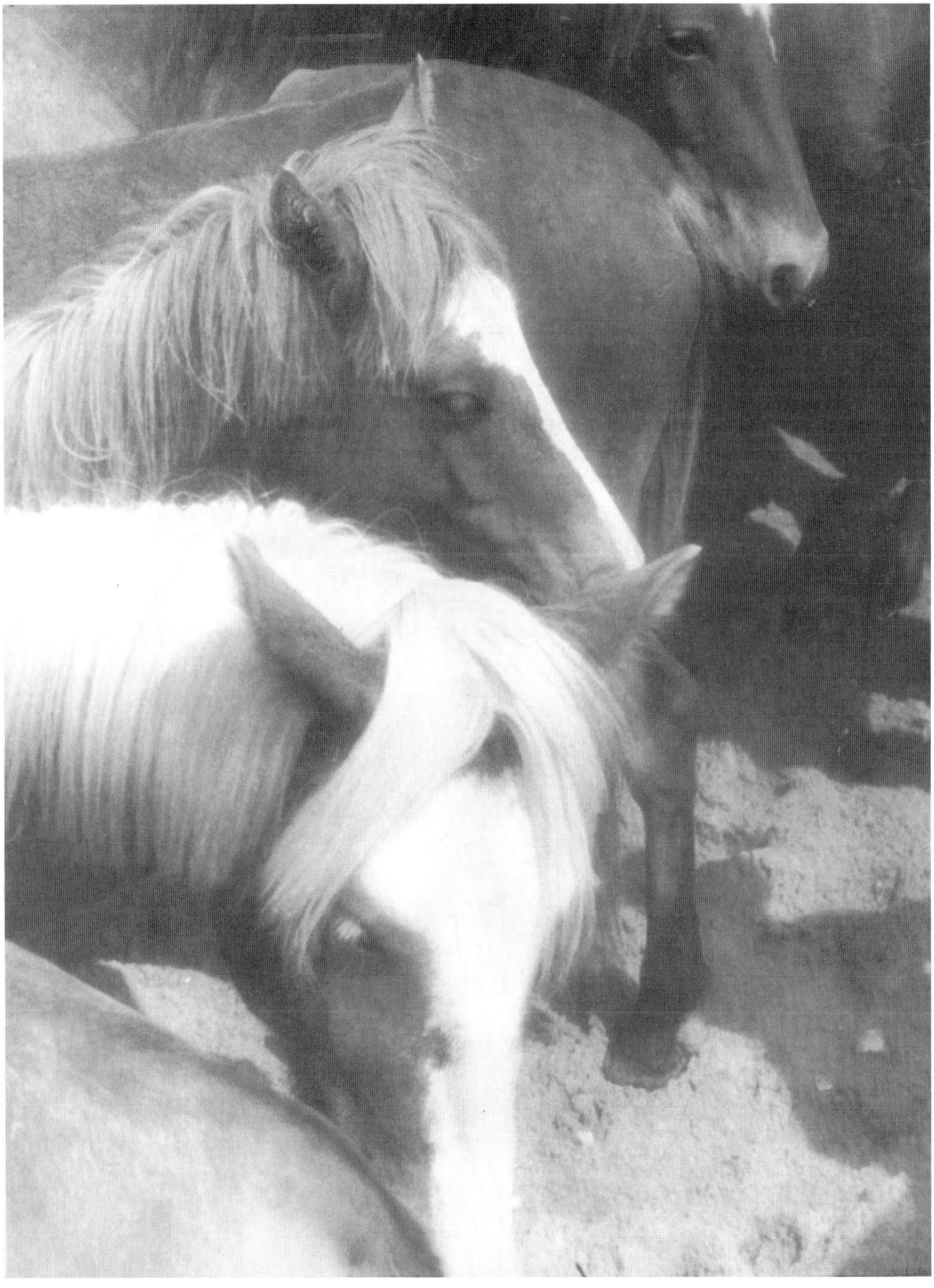

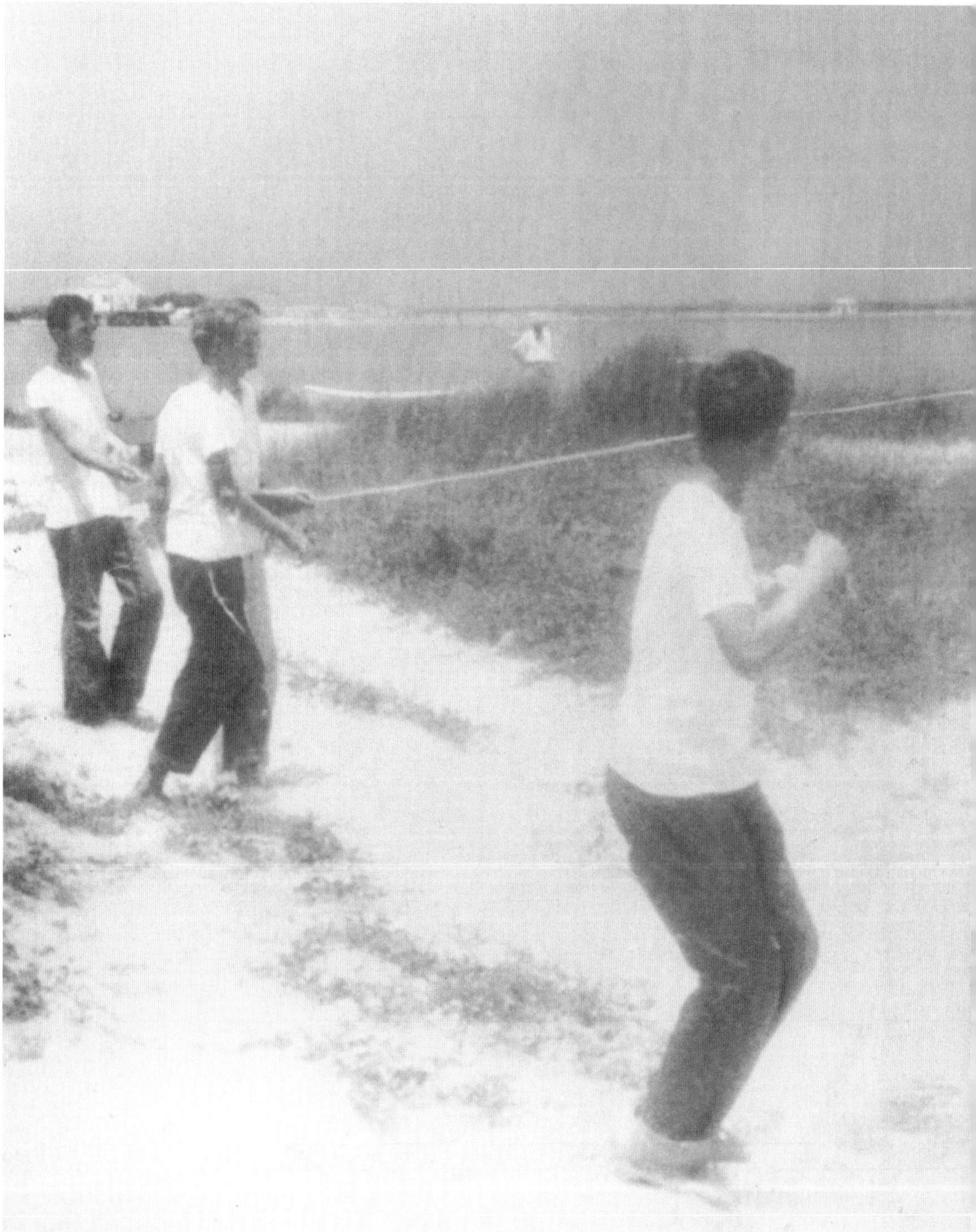

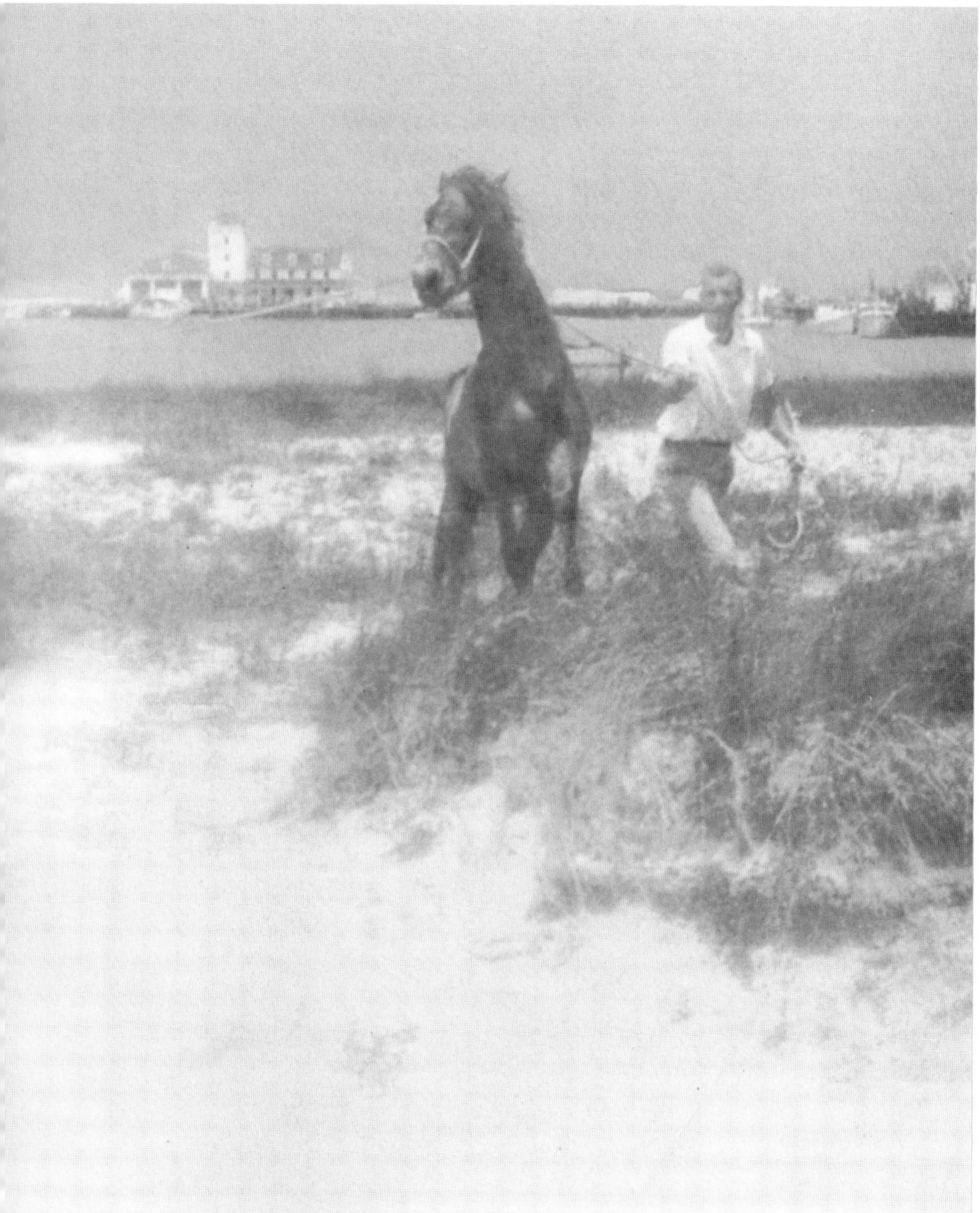

above a confusion of bays, sorrels, and chestnuts packed tightly into the small corral. The lasso settled around the neck of a rough-coated colt that was sticking as close to Mother as possible.

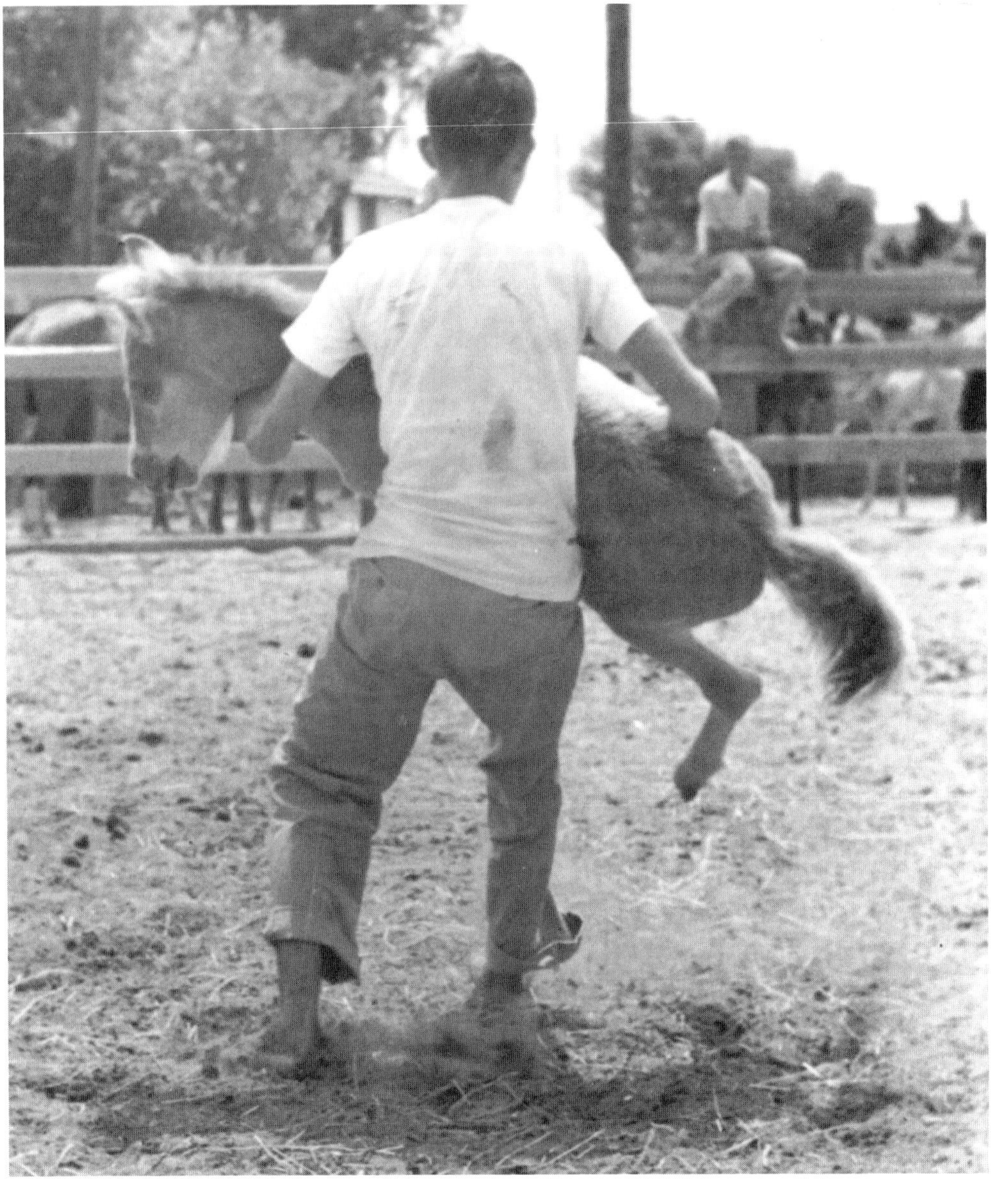

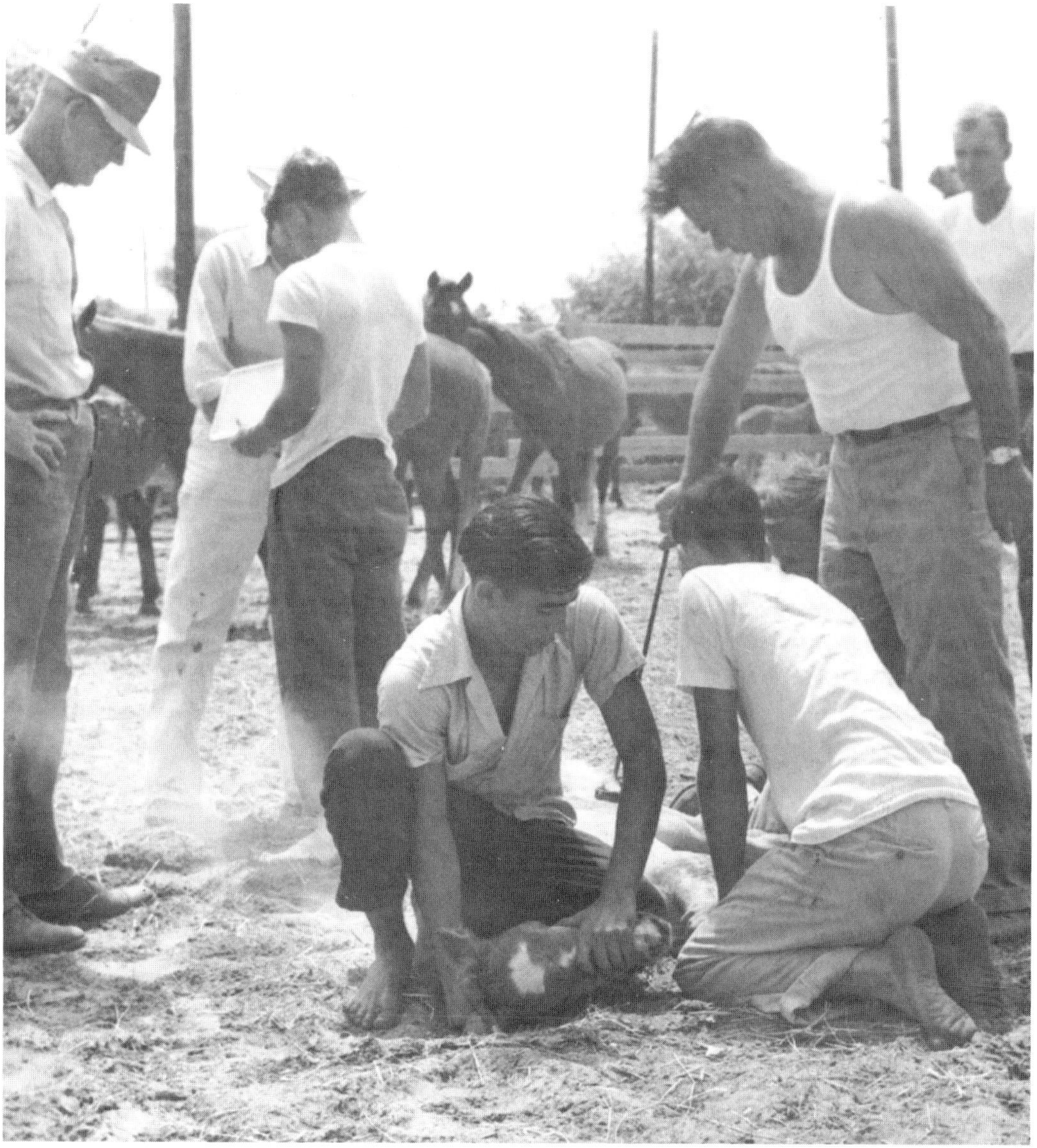

How terrified the colts were of the branding!

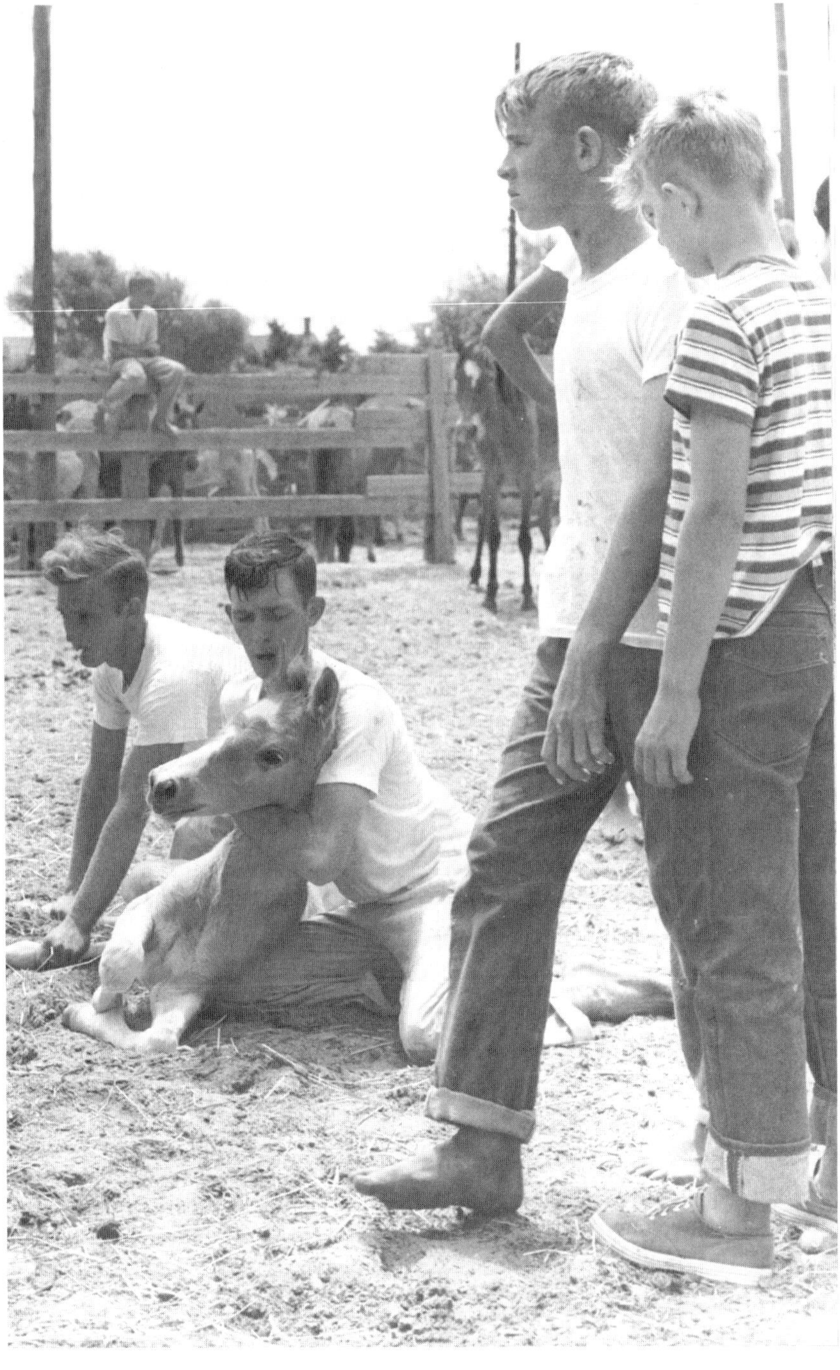

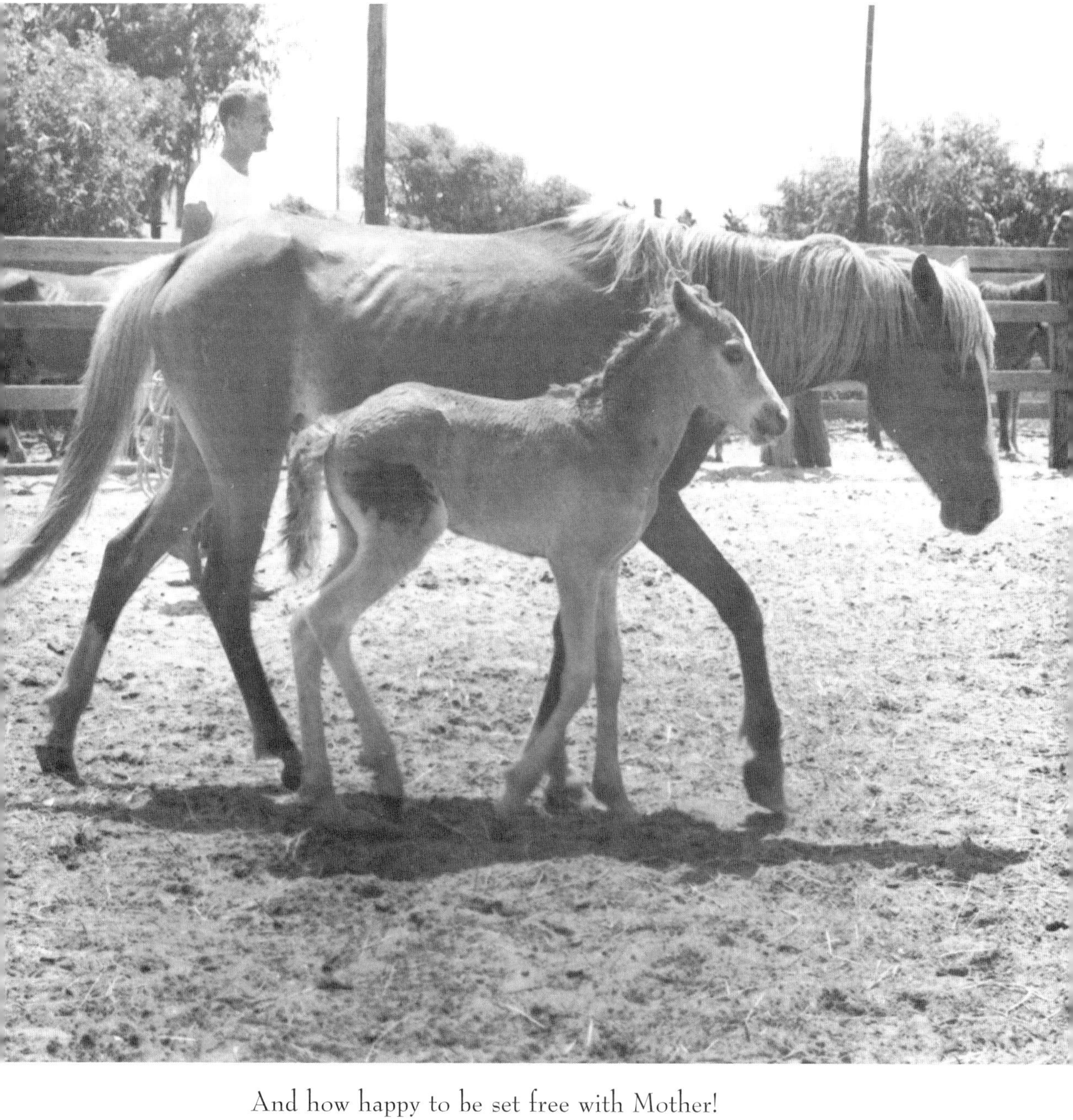

And how happy to be set free with Mother!

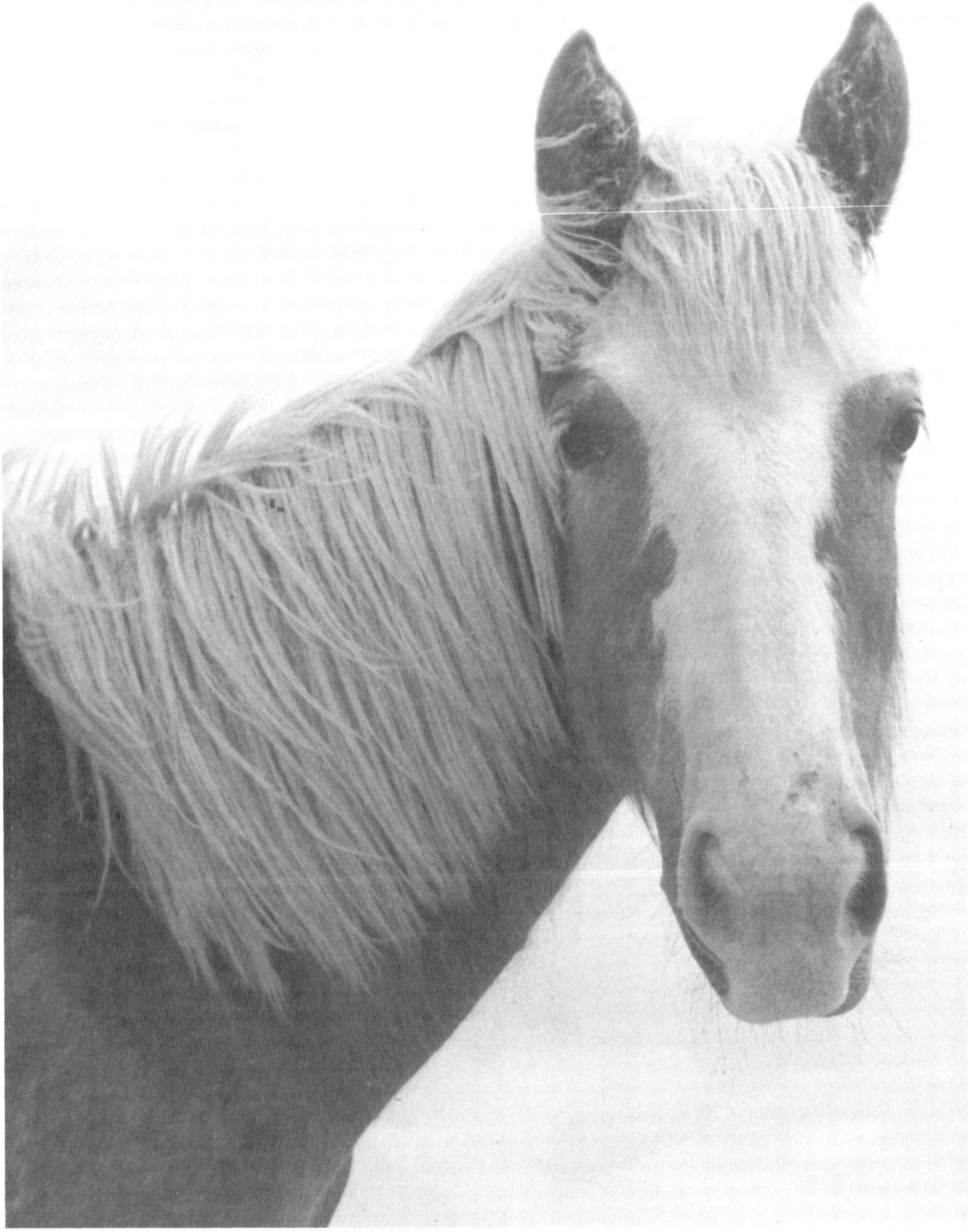

After the roundup, the ponies scattered for another year to wander the island as they pleased. You might have met one strolling down a village lane or cooling off in the shade of the Community Store. They were not so much wild as free, their only restraint the picket fences built not to keep the horses in but to keep them out—out of yards, gardens, and garbage cans.

Today, the ponies are gone except for a handful that are penned in a small range on the sound. The Park Service has banished them to a small reserve because the horses ate the island's newly planted dune grass before it could take hold. The ponies are gone from their open range, but the fences still run through the town.

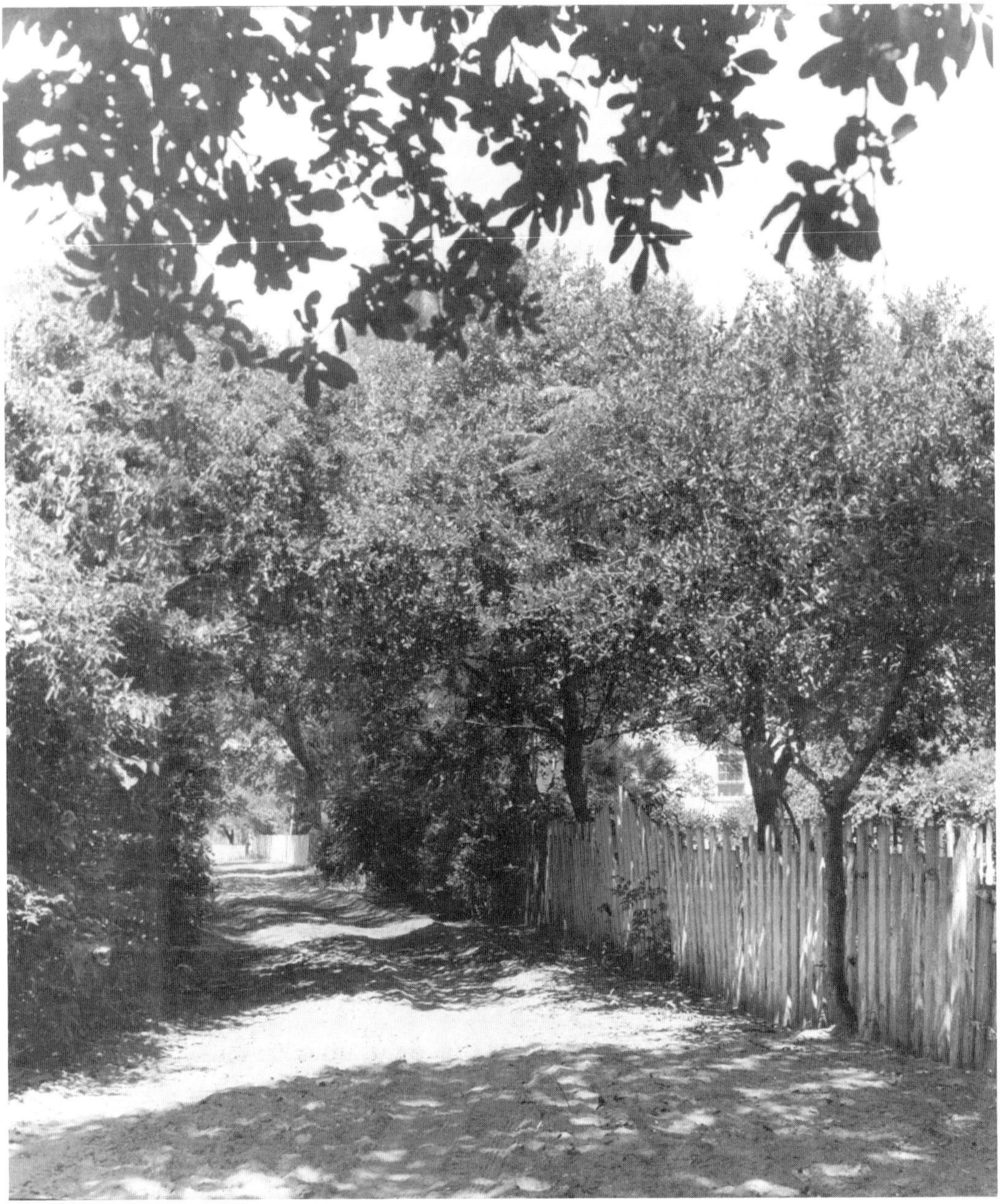

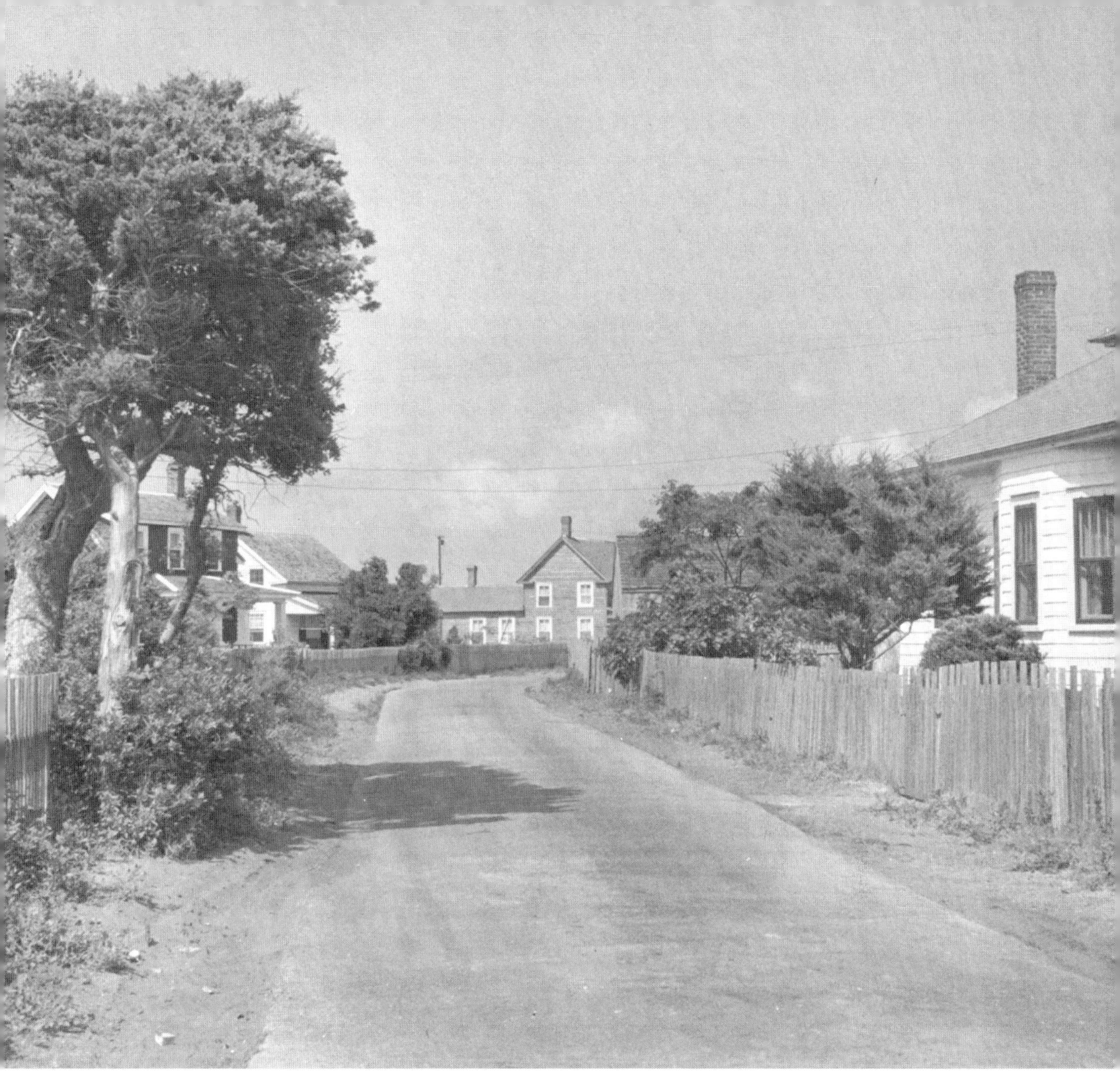

The fences protect neat houses and yards rich with oleander bushes and hydrangeas. Outside the fences are phlox, morning glory, and the earth-red "Joe Bell" flowers that grow wild.

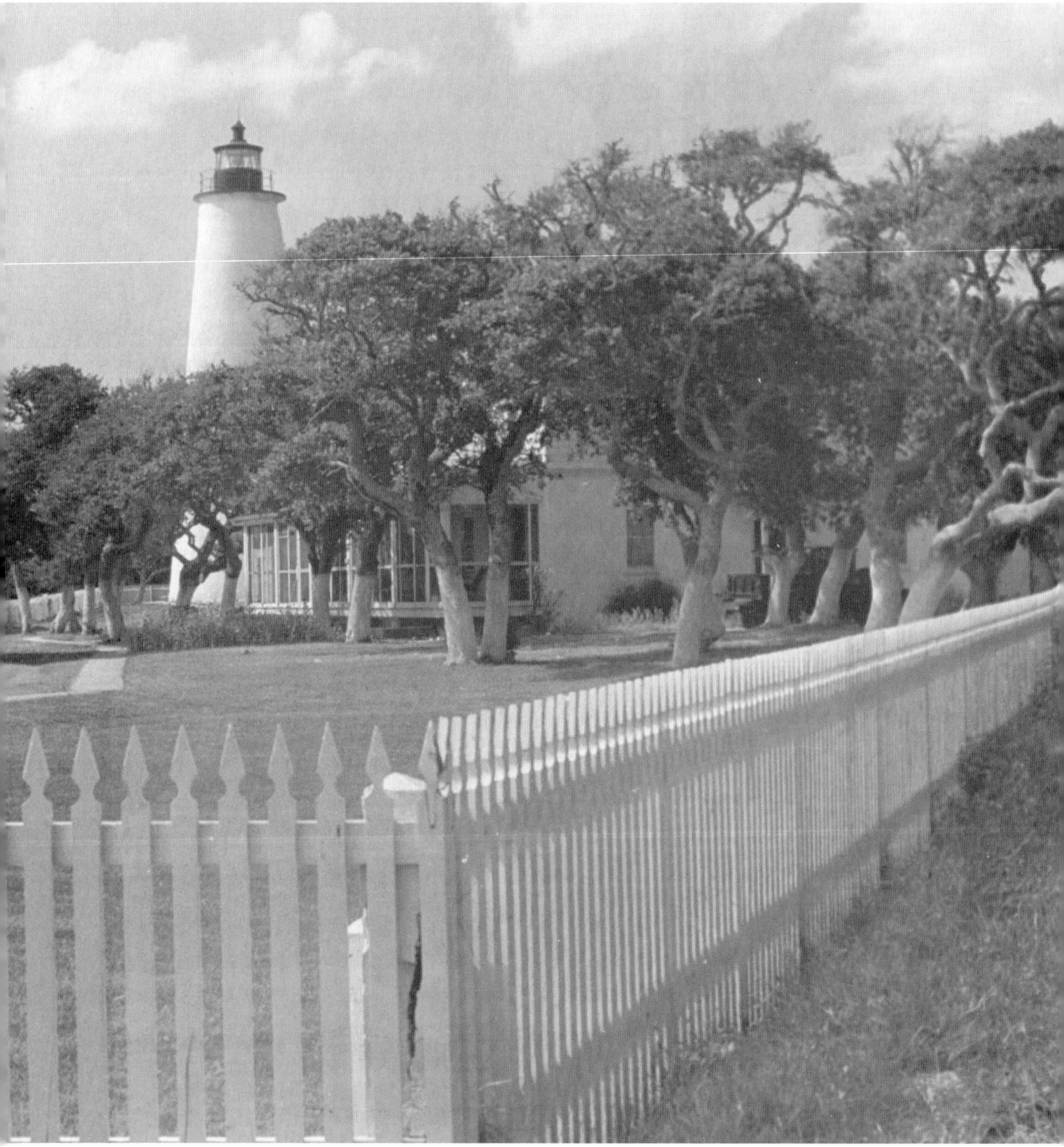

Another fence encloses the tidy lighthouse grounds, the carved pickets gleaming white. Other fences have grayed liked driftwood, which is what they have nearly become.

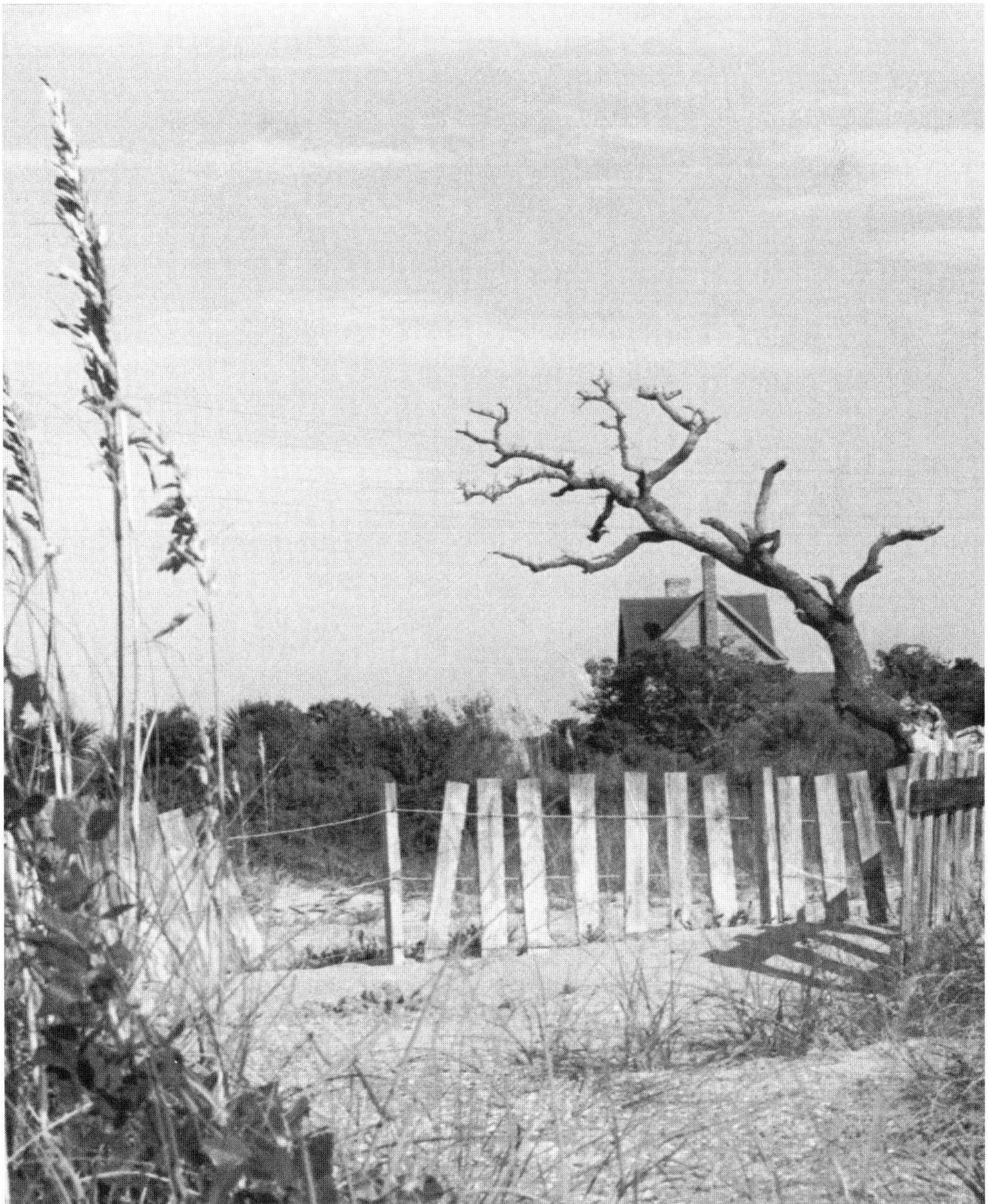

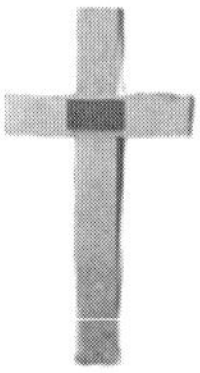

Fences stand guard around the graveyards of Ocracoke—small, personal plots often situated just beyond the backyards of the houses where the people they honor lived and died.

Funerals are simple and moving. The expenses are paid by the community burial association, to which members contribute one-fourth of the expense when a neighbor or relative dies. There are as many relatives as neighbors because of intermarriage through the centuries on this isolated strip of sand.

The old stones lean in the sandy soil. Below one lies Ann Howard, born in 1724 and laid to rest in 1841, some 117 years following her birth.

Then there was Job Wahab, whose headstone states firmly that he was born in 1885 and died in 1842, forty-three years before his birth. This seems unlikely even for Ocracoke. Some careless stonecutter made a mistake, and no one hurried to return the stone to the mainland to be corrected. The islanders seldom do anything in a hurry.

There is now a new community cemetery, and some of the old graveyards are disappearing in tangles of weeds and bushes.

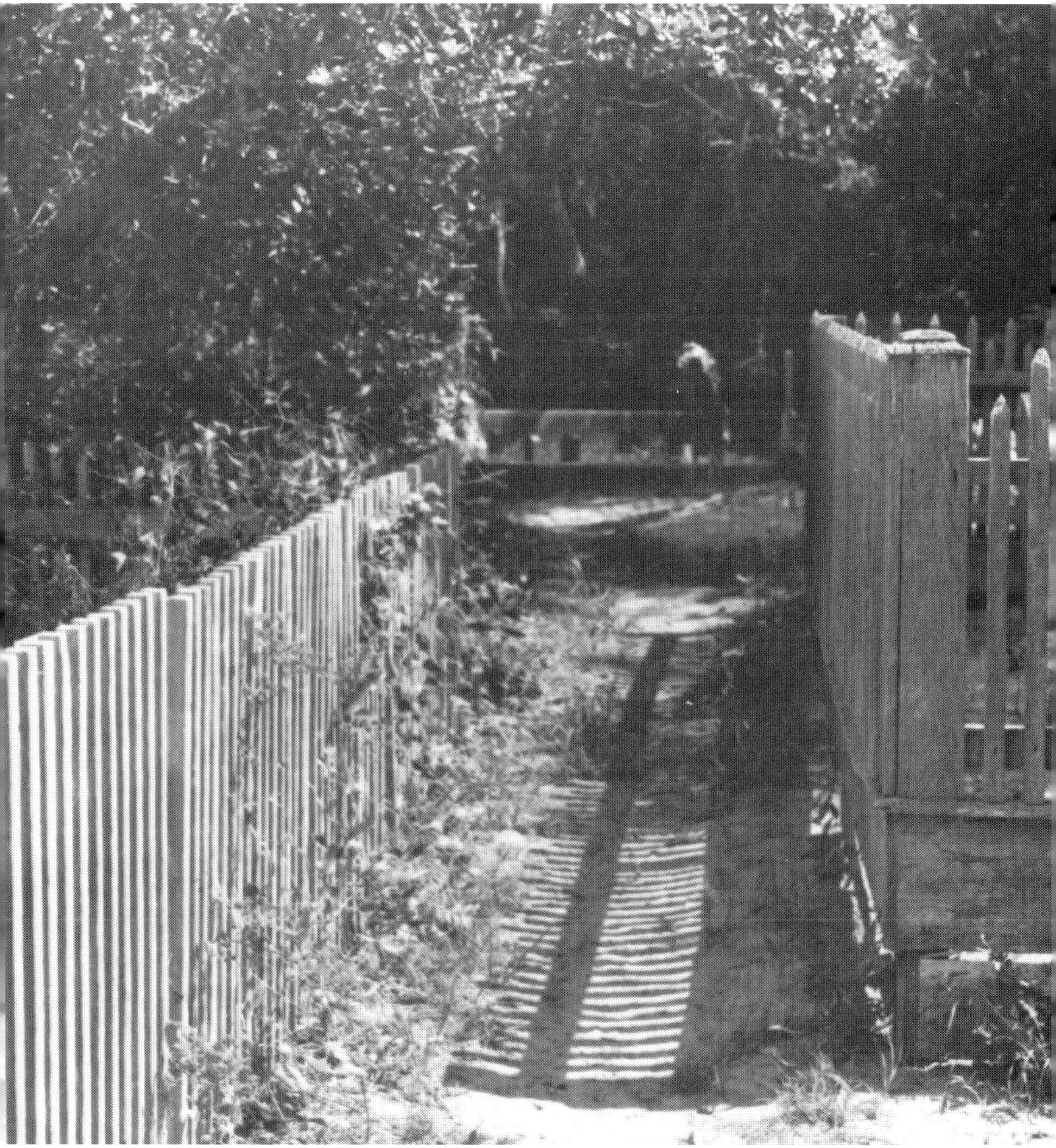

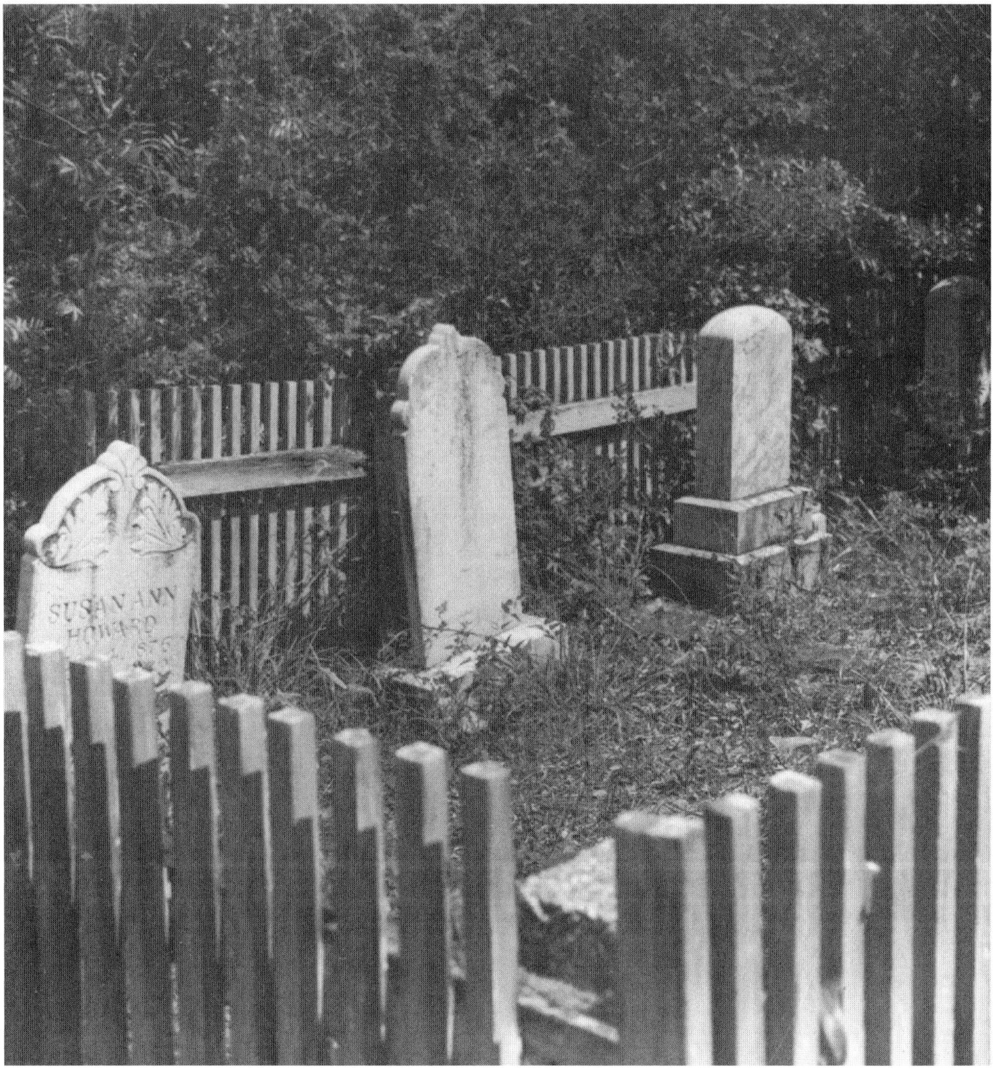
SUSAN ANN
HOWARD

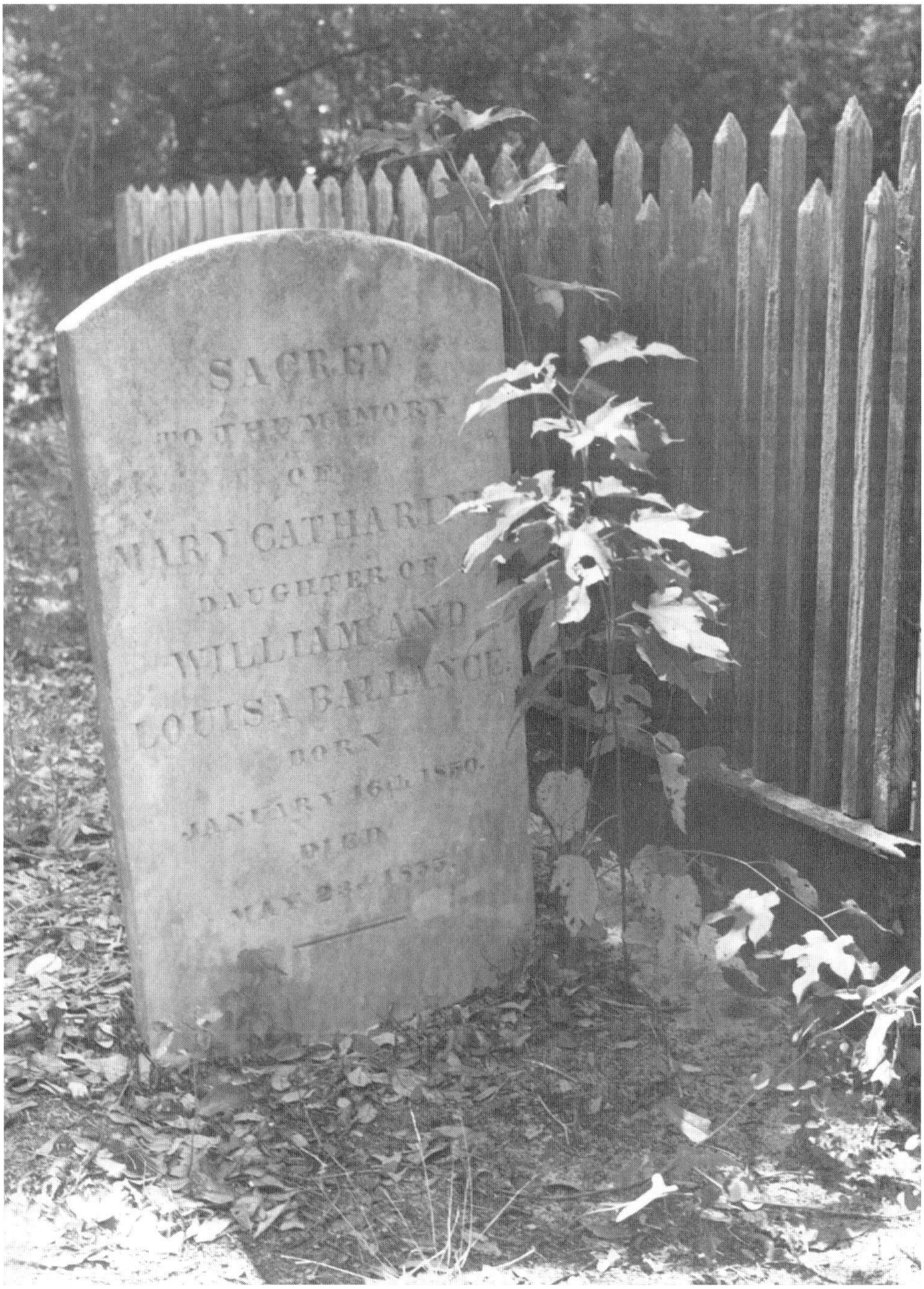
SACRED
DAUGHTER OF
WILLIAM AND
LOUISA BALLANCE.
BORN
DIED

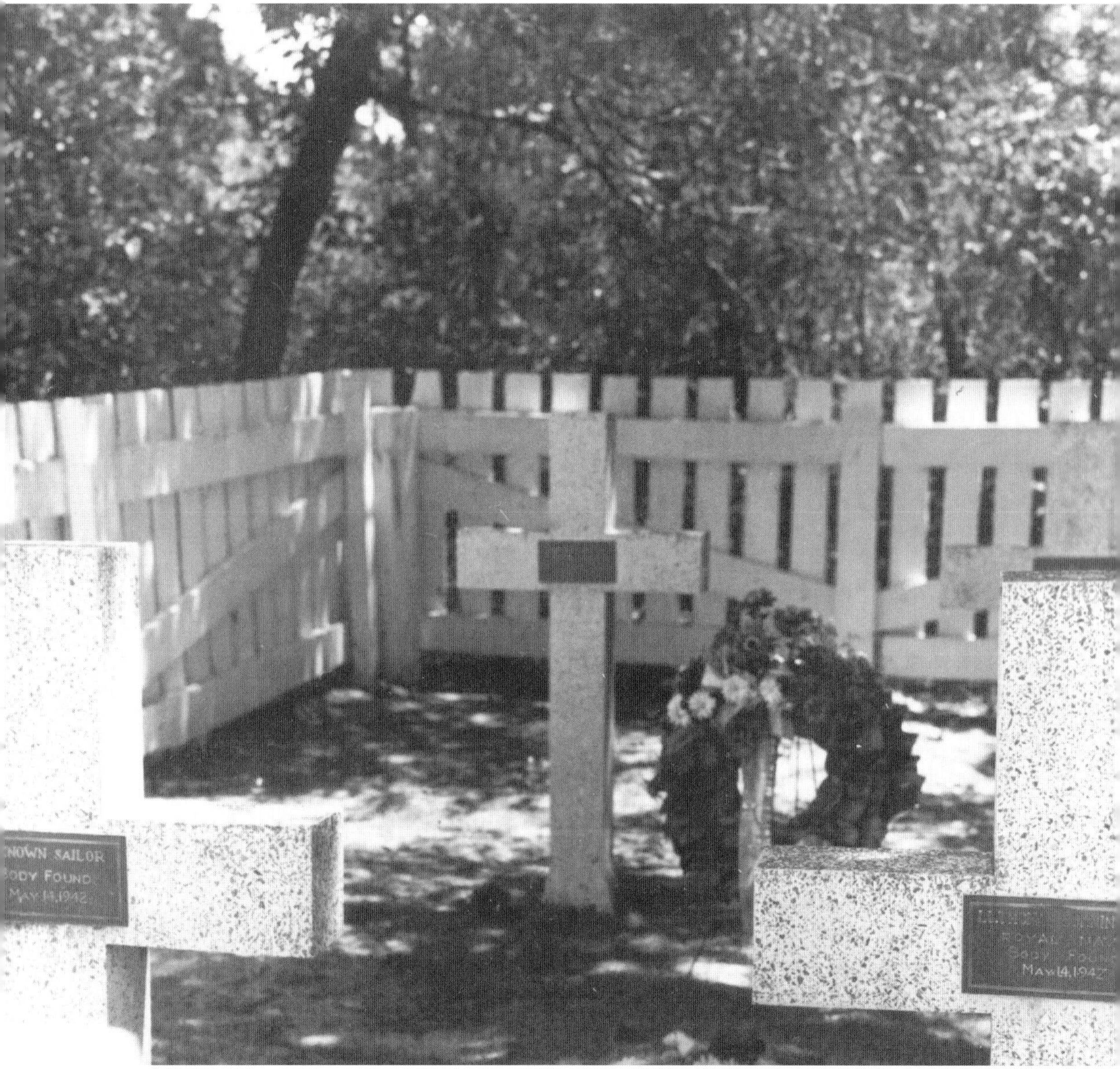
NOWN SAILOR
BODY FOUND
MAY 14, 1942
MAY 14, 1942

No weeds encroach on the small square of land known as the British Cemetery, its fence trim and white. Here lie Lieutenant Thomas Cunningham and three other crew members of the HMS *Bedfordshire*, sunk by a German submarine in 1942. The four bodies, two of them never identified, washed ashore on Ocracoke. The islanders buried them, put up headstones, and fenced the graves to thwart straying ponies. The islanders found the known sailors' families in England, and today a plaque on the gate quotes the British poet Rupert Brooke:

> If I should die, think only this of me:
> That there's some corner of a foreign field
> That is forever England.

For the men of the *Bedfordshire*, their English corner of a foreign field is a well-tended little graveyard in the shade of the cedars and yaupon of Ocracoke.

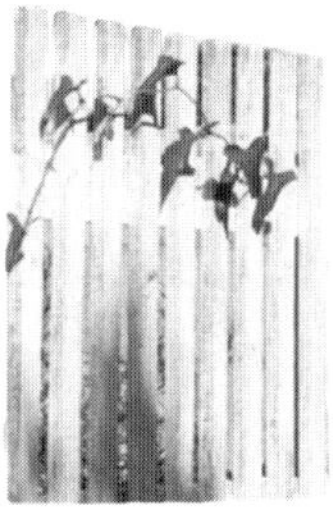

Beyond another sun-dappled fence, you can glimpse the cross on Ocracoke's Methodist church. Once, there were a Southern Methodist and a Northern Methodist church. The congregations decided to unite, but no one could decide which building to use. So what did they do but tear down two perfectly good churches and from the remains erect a new church, about which no one could argue.

Near the lighthouse is another church, the Assembly of God.

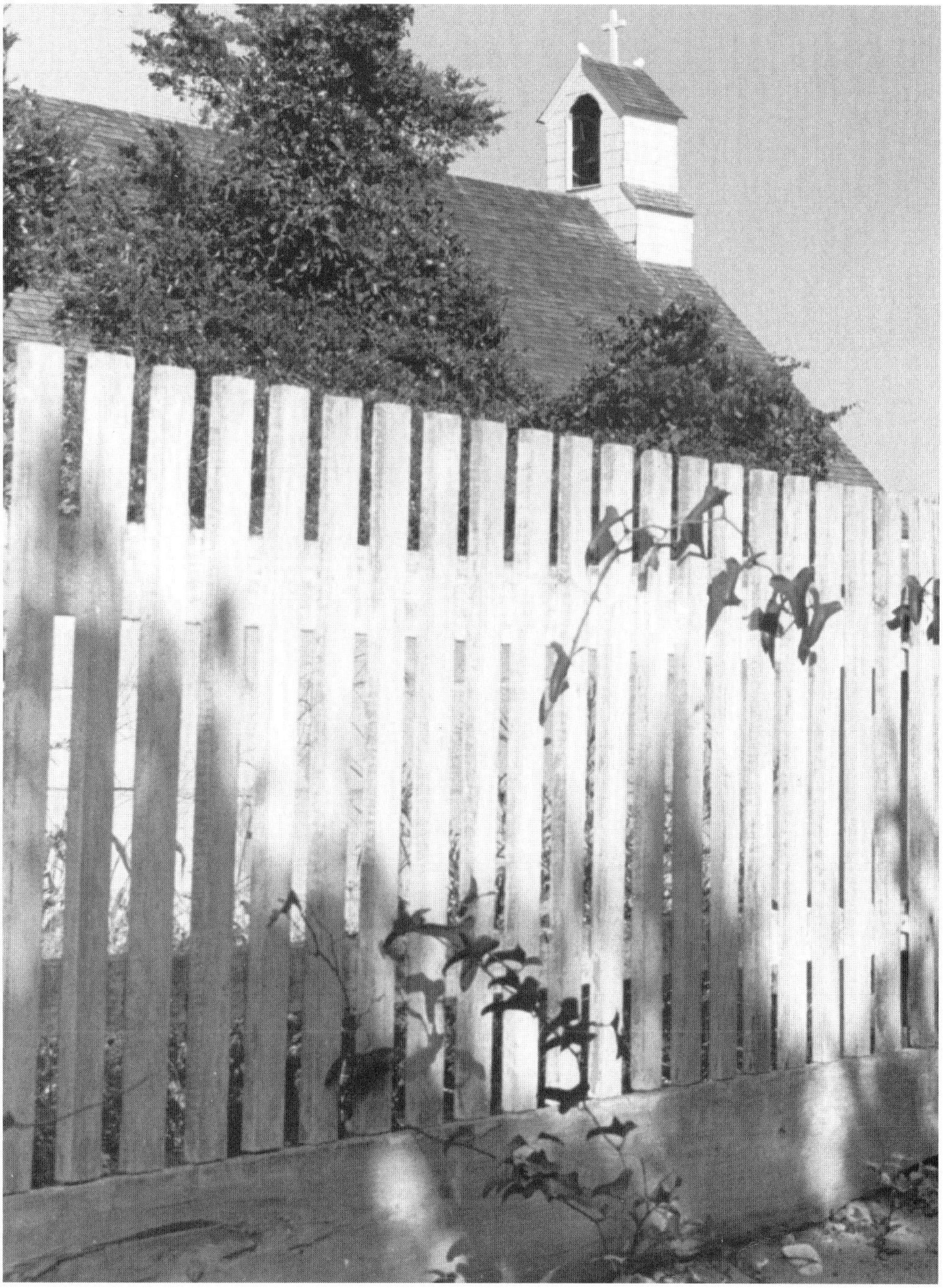

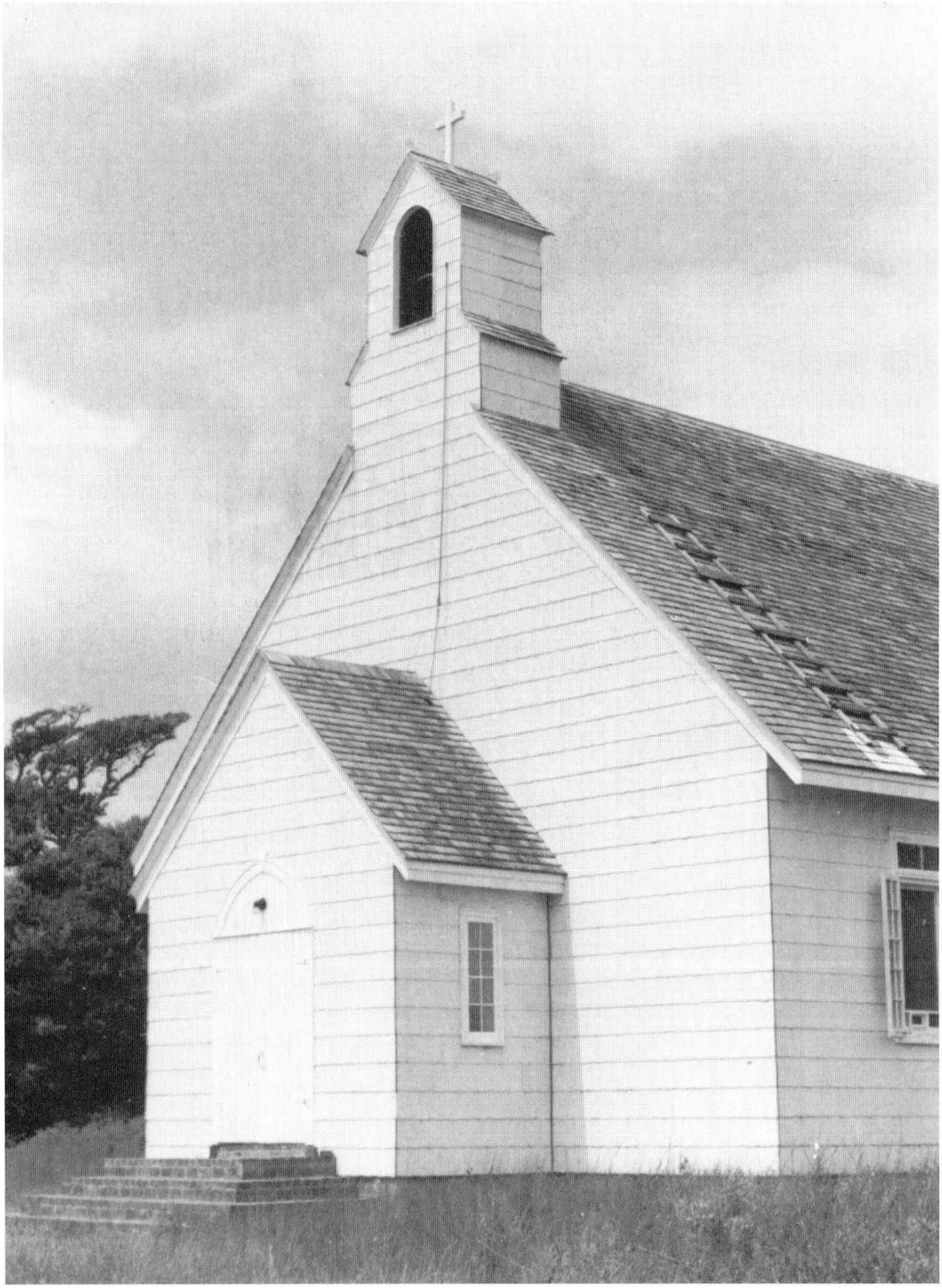

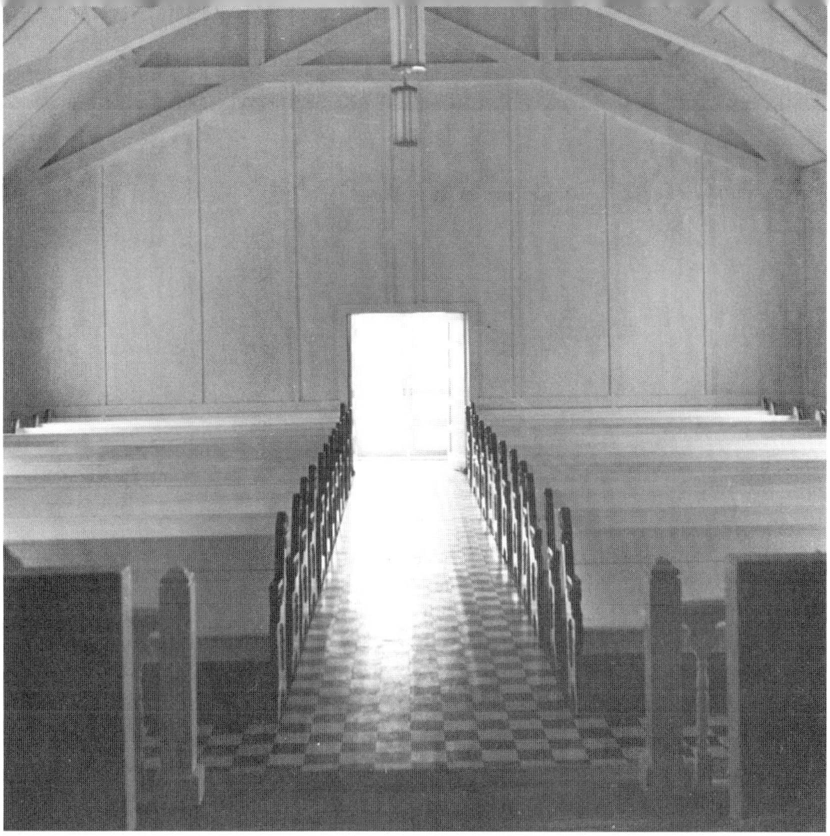

There never have been any fences around this church, not even to keep the ponies at a distance. The building is as simple and unadorned as a ship. Inside is the same spick-and-span plainness, from the rafters of the white ceiling to the shining black-trimmed benches.

This is the church of a seafaring people, and the wooden cross on the altar came from the sea. It was made from the spar of a sunken ship, and this is its story.

In the early days of World War II, Captain Bill Gaskill had a son who was in the Merchant Marine. James Gaskill's ship was the *Caribsea*, an East Coast cargo vessel. One day, a cousin walking on the Atlantic beach found part of a cabin wall with a framed second mate's certificate mounted upon it. It was still legible, and it was that of his cousin James Gaskill. The next day, a spar marked with the name of the *Caribsea* washed ashore on Ocracoke from the waters of Pamlico Sound at a spot near Captain Bill Gaskill's own pier. The spar had floated through Ocracoke Inlet and up the sound before coming to rest at the very place where James Gaskill had lived as a child.

It was not until later that James's parents were officially notified of their son's death. The cross made from the spar of the *Caribsea* stands on the altar in memory of still another islander claimed by the sea.

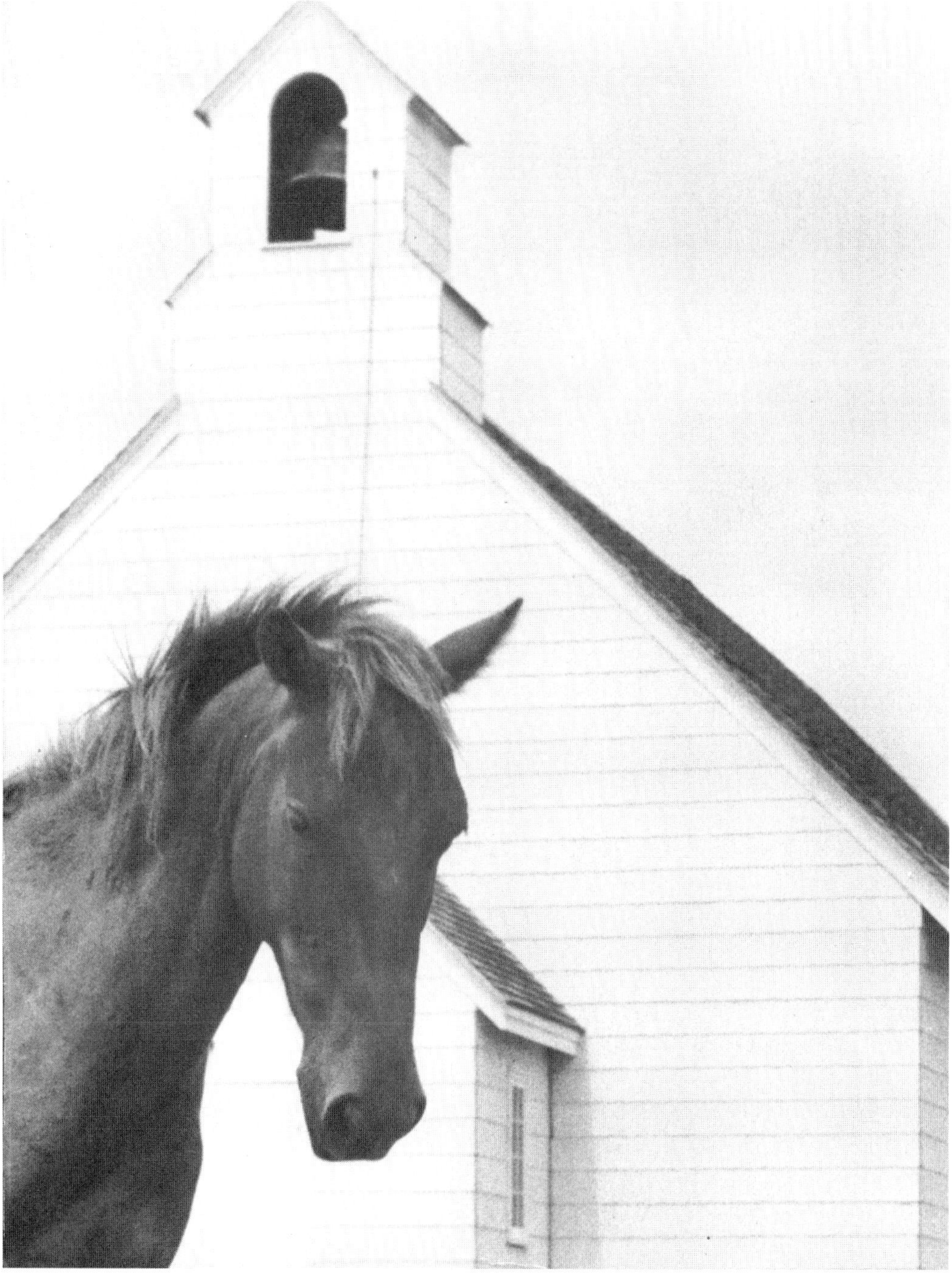

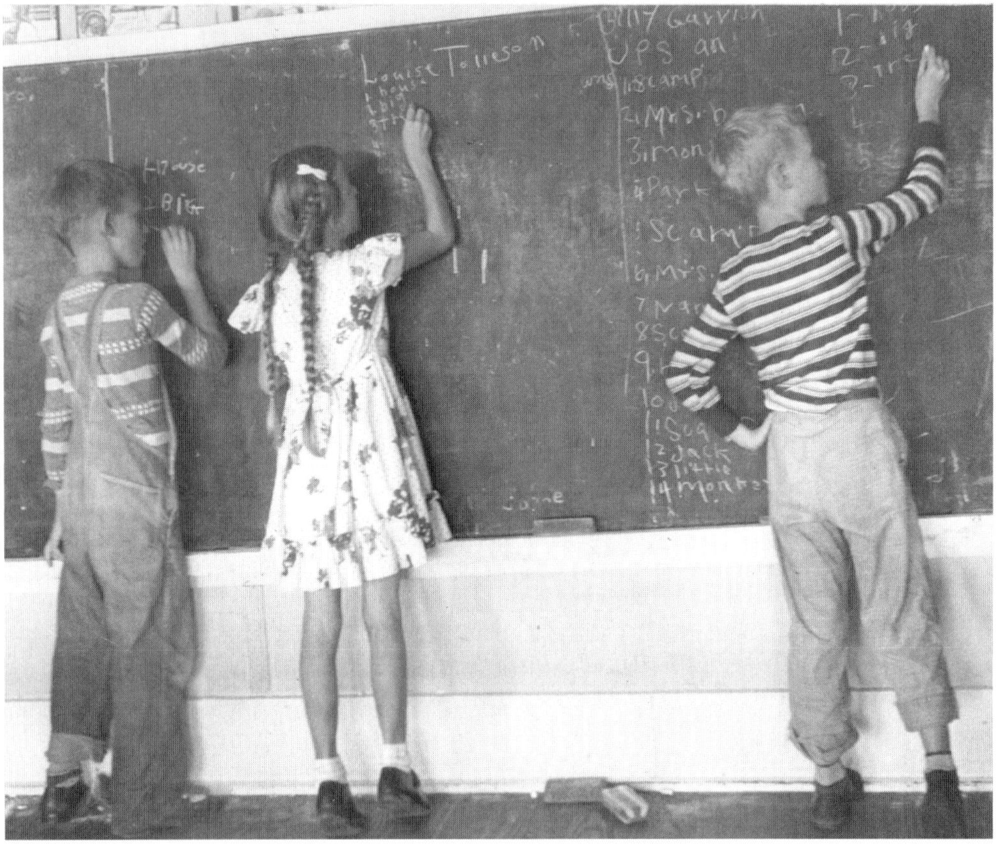

Ocracoke has had a school since 1808. The present one is a one-story white frame building. In front of it stands Alice Rondthaler. She and her husband, Theodore, fine teachers from the mainland, came planning to spend a year and stayed for fifteen to teach the children of Ocracoke. They have been an energetic and helpful part of the community.

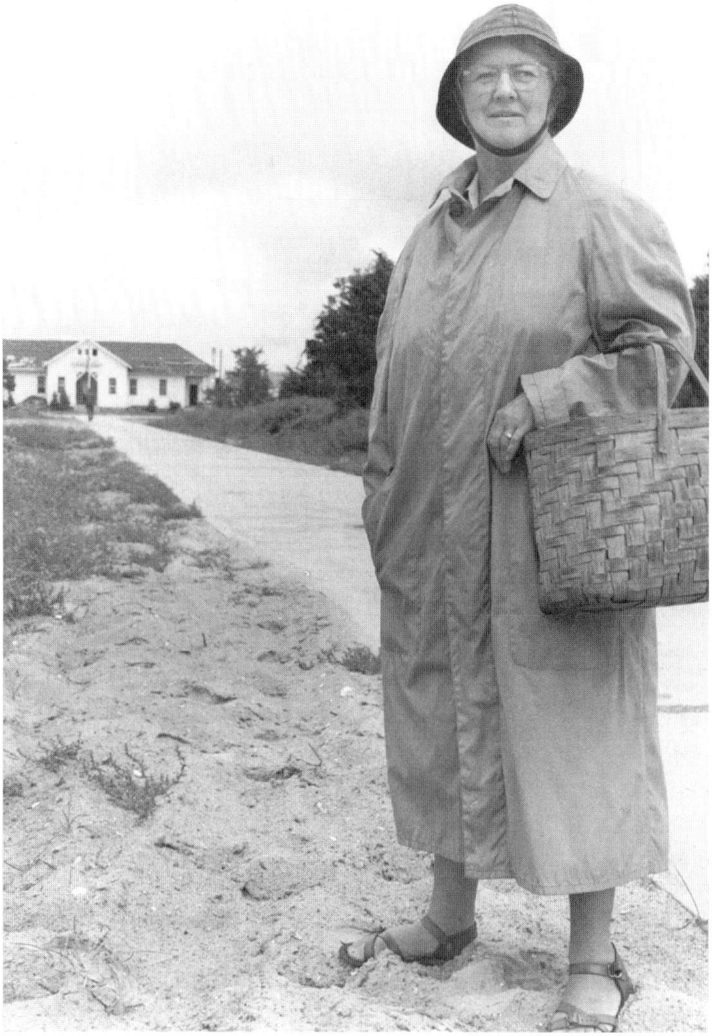

Devoted teachers and an active and interested PTA have created a good school. Many mainland problems do not apply here. There is no overcrowding. Every child can walk to school, so buses and school lunches are not needed. And how many other children can study where the distant murmur of the sea drifts into the classroom?

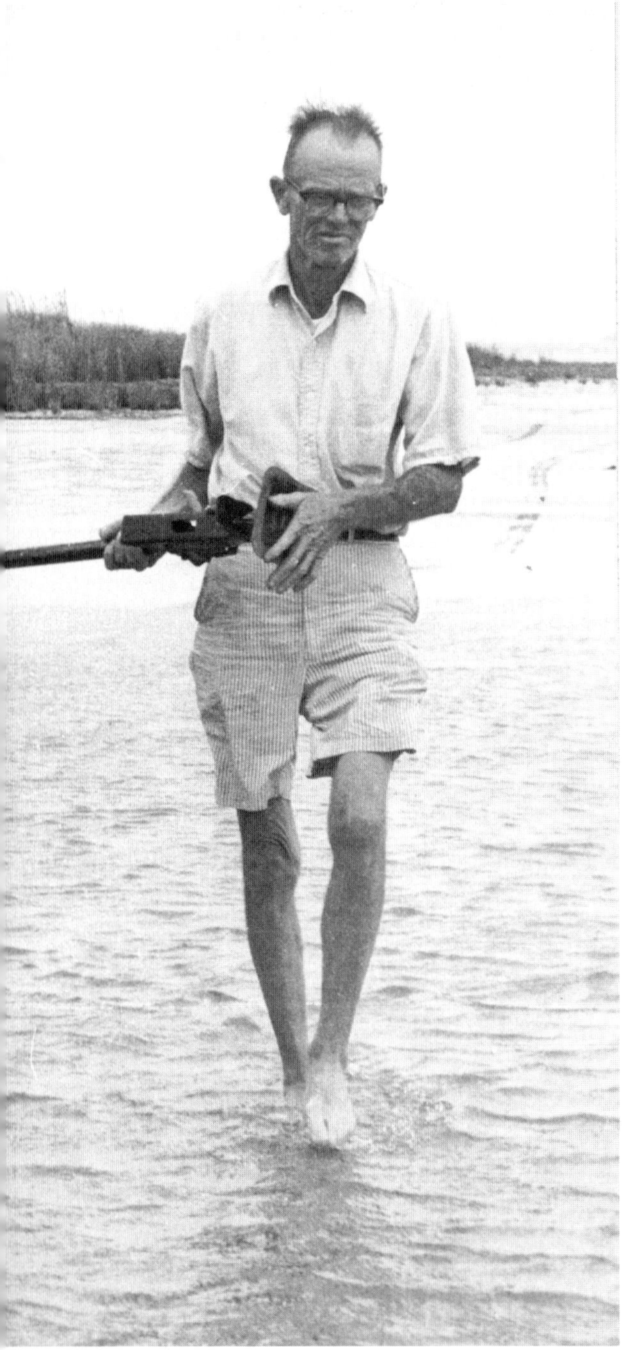

Ocracoke is inhabited by a hardy, courteous, independent people. About 170 families adding up to 500 or 600 people, close-knit through years of intermarriage and self-sufficiency, go their hardworking but leisurely way. They are friendly but unimpressed by names or celebrity. Given good reason, they will ignore anyone.

The names you find in eighteenth-century records are still the island's names—Bragg, Gaskins, Howard, O'Neal, Jackson, Styron, Wade, Williams, and Wahab.

They sprang from shipwrecked colonists, English seamen, runaway bonded servants, perhaps a pirate or two, but mostly from settlers from the Carolina and Virginia mainland. Though mainly of English blood, their background includes traces of other nationalities. In fact, the Wahabs boast a full-blooded Arab great-great-great-great-grandfather who washed ashore on an oar.

The island speech is special, too. It has its own idioms, pronunciations, and cadence. People say that it is like that of Devon, or north-country England, in the time of Elizabeth I. Certainly, it has a Cockney trace. High tide is *hoigh toide*. A *v* can be a *w*, as in the *wictim* of a wreck. But old words like *tote* and *fetch* and all of the old patterns of speech that preceded the American Revolution are disappearing as contacts with the outside world increase. Soon, there will be an Ocracoke generation whose members sound just like everyone else.

In 1795, there were only thirty families on the island, and their income came from piloting ships through Ocracoke Inlet. They lived on Pamlico Sound, near their work, away from the fury of the ocean. With the end of piloting, they turned to fishing, hunting, the tilling of small gardens, raising stock on a range that never had to be fenced, and working in the Lifesaving Service. Later came commercial fishing, shrimping, and the Coast Guard.

Islanders have always had to cope with a multitude of chores. The people of Ocracoke built their own boats and their houses. Much of their lumber—oak and mahogany, cedar and teak—was salvaged from wrecks. Today, more ordinary lumber is imported from the mainland.

Life was simple on Ocracoke. Neighbor helped neighbor, and everyone lent a hand on community projects. There was no crime. Where could a criminal hide? No one ever locked a door. But with the stream of strangers now passing through, some are beginning to rethink the need. The old ways are changing. The speech is changing. Square dancing has ended.

You can no longer hear ponies' hooves pounding in the night or find horses in the streets. Yet the essential qualities of the people have not been lost.

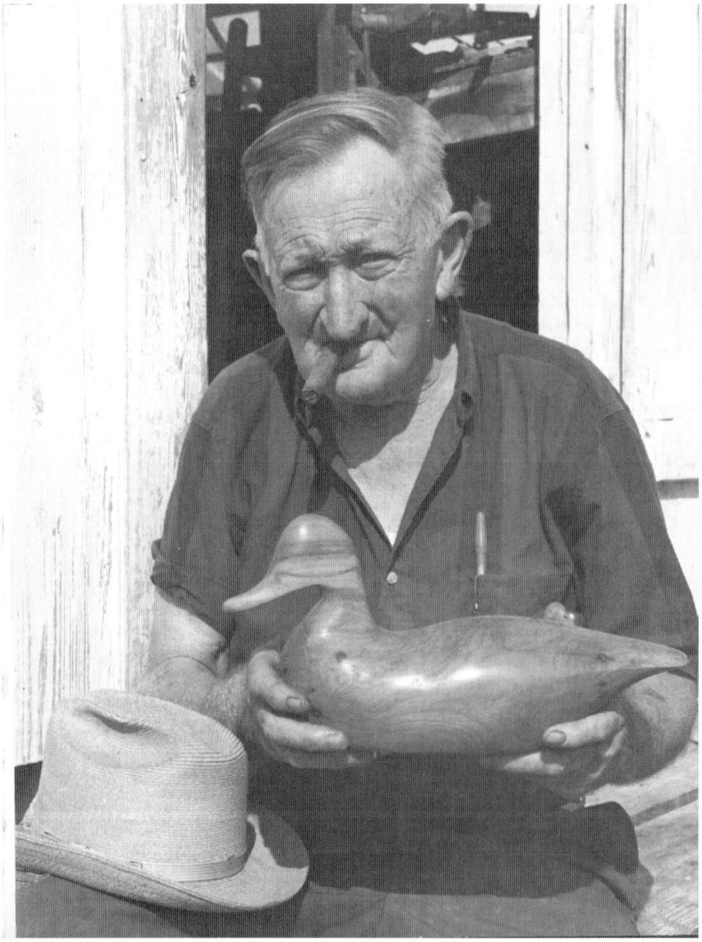

Charlie McWilliams, retired now, stays busy carving beautiful birds from native wood. For years, "Charlie Mac" drove the island's mail bus from Hatteras down the backbreaking route along Ocracoke's lonely dunes.

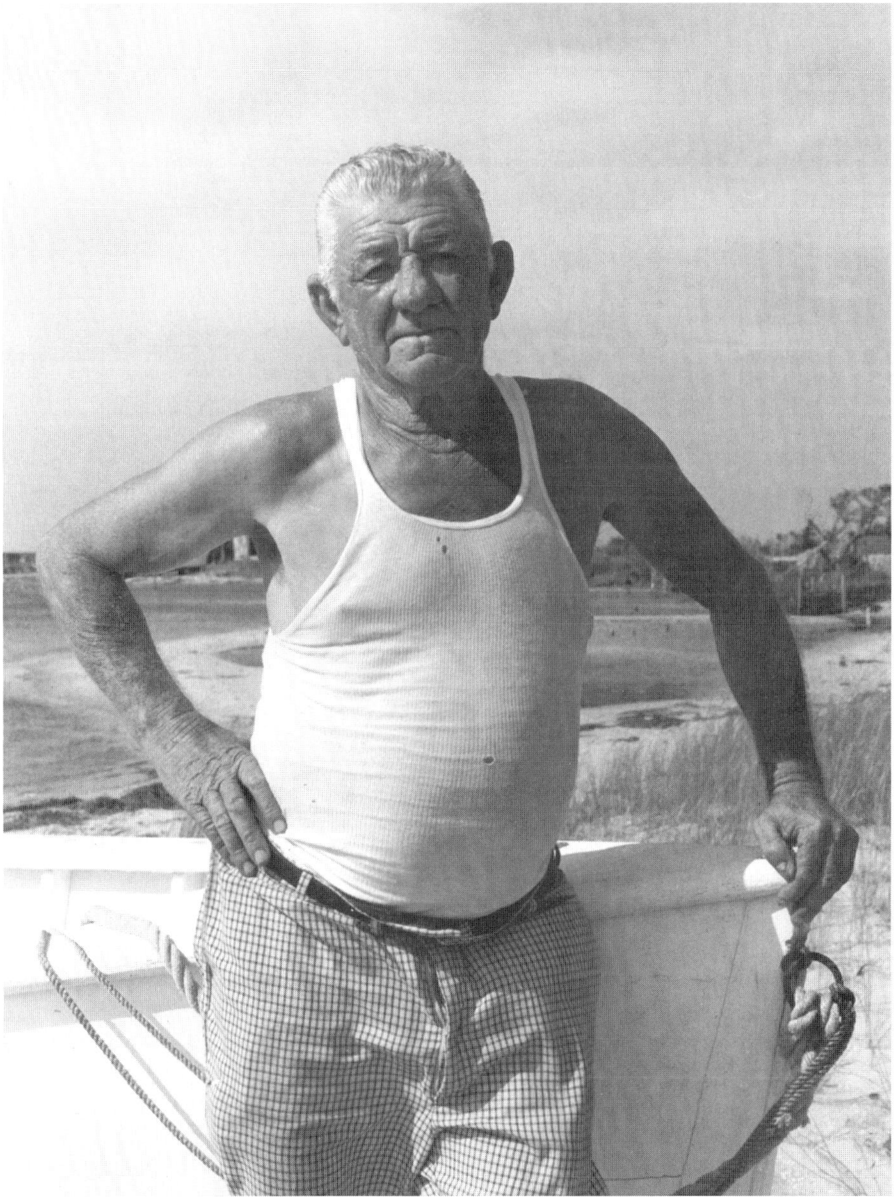

Harry O'Neal, carpenter, jack-of-all-trades, and father of eleven sons

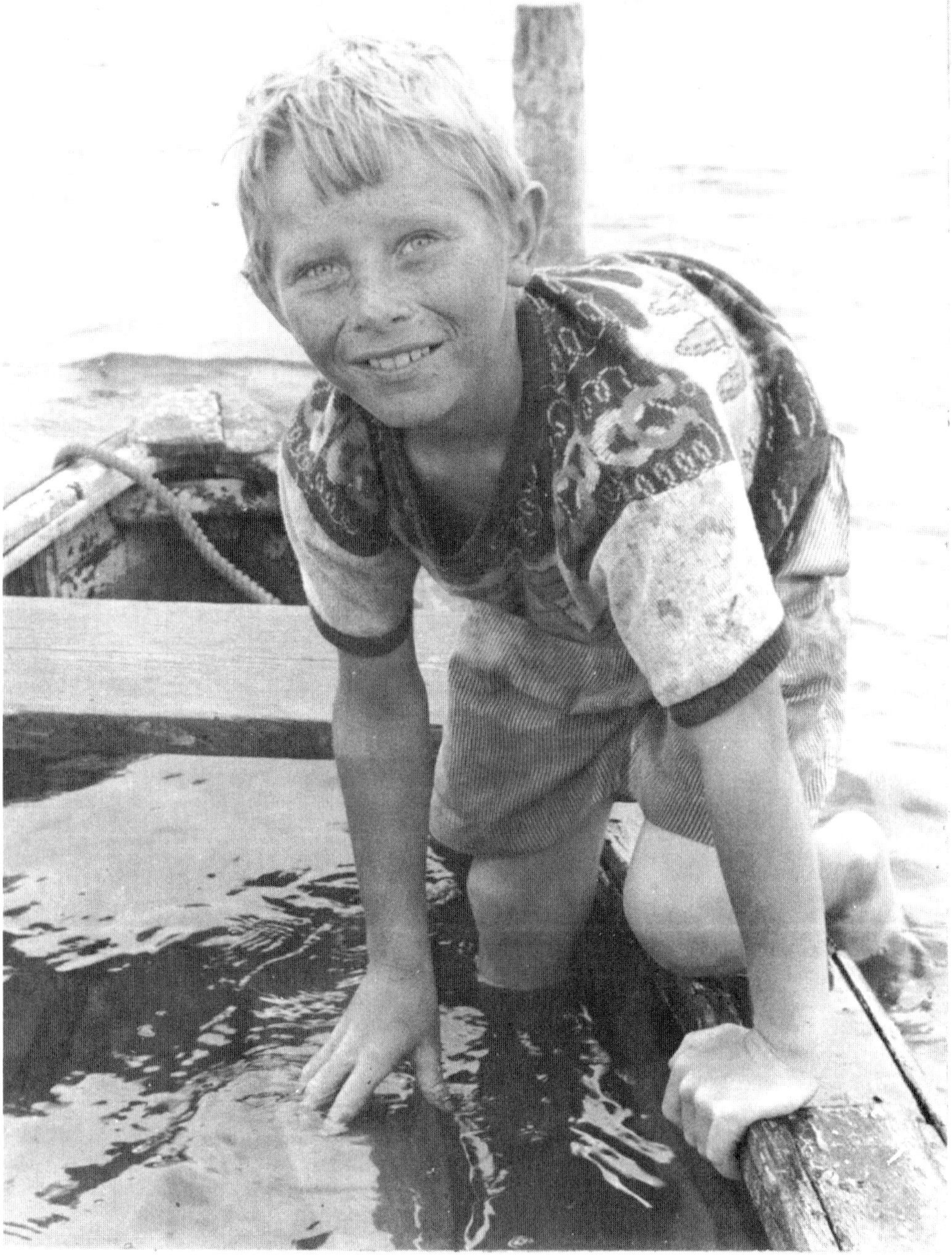

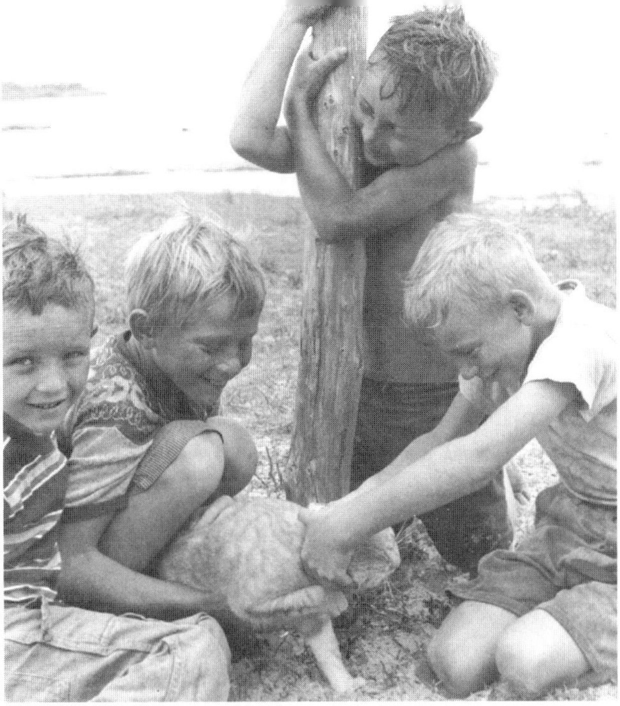

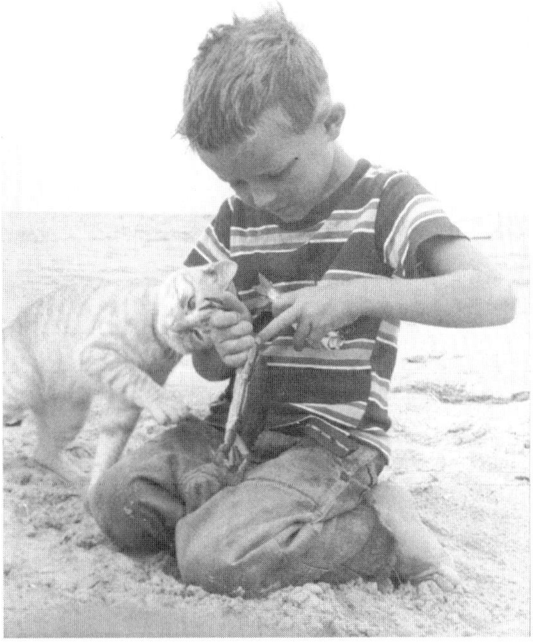

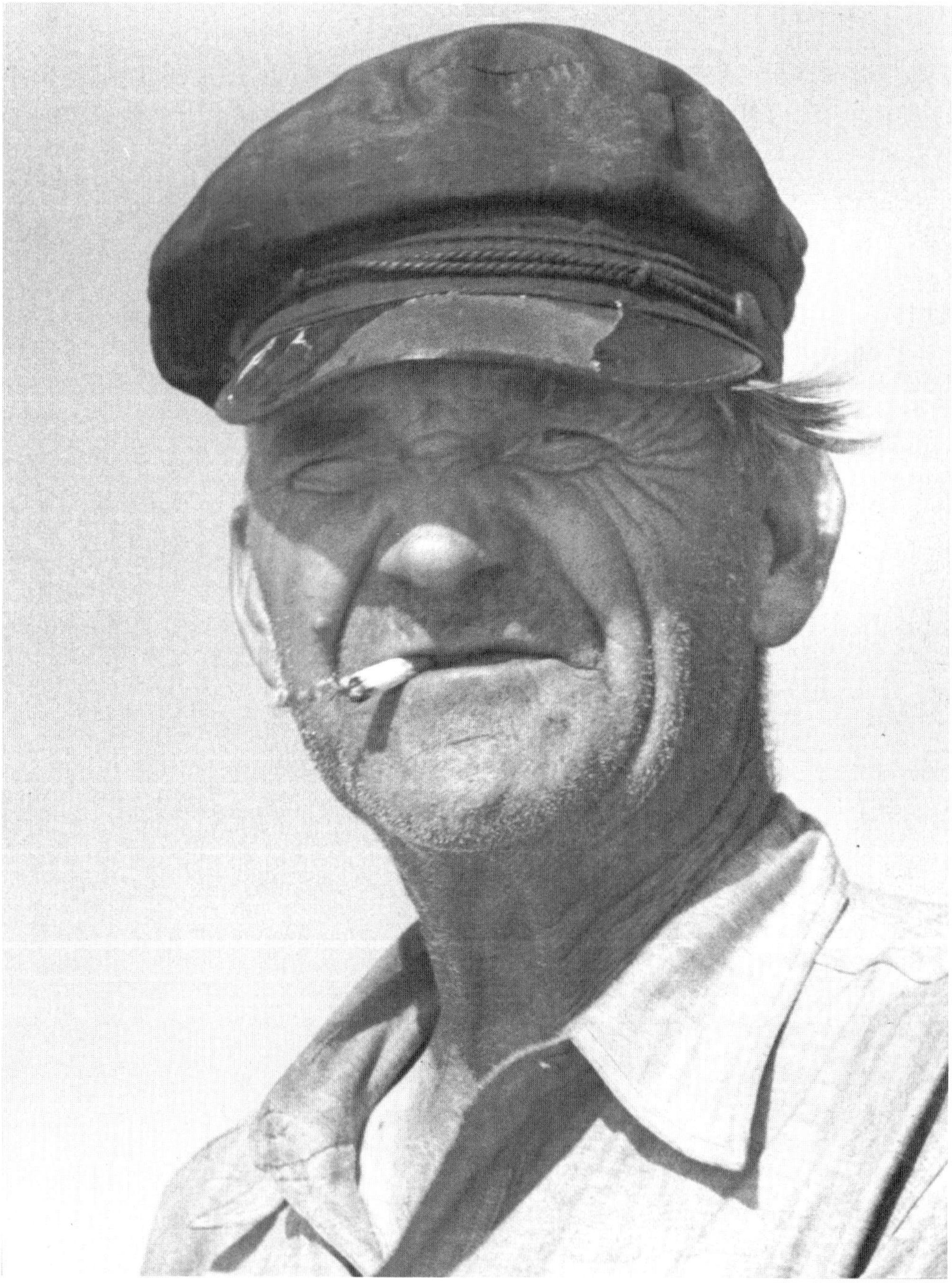

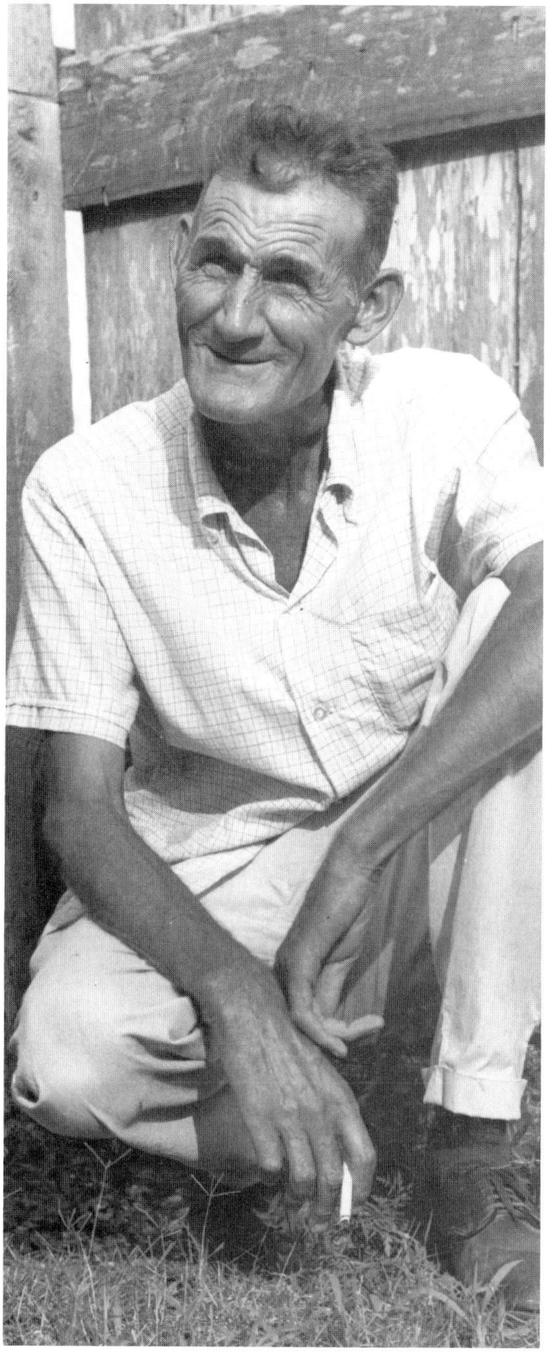

Jake **Alligood** was not born on Ocracoke but was very much a part of it, he and his son, Jake—Big Jake and Little Jake. Big Jake was your man if you had surf fishing on your mind. He'd furnish transportation, bait, and advice. He had an uncanny ability to find the holes where the fish were biting. Perhaps it was a knowledge of wind and tide and the actions of the birds. Governors, senators, and famous sportsmen were among his clients, but none got better service or attention than did the lowliest amateur fisherman. Even when he grew nearly blind and had to depend upon

Little Jake, he could find the fish. Perhaps he could smell them. Big Jake was a fine mechanic, too. Blind, he could hear what was wrong with a motor and fix it by the feel of his hands.

Big Jake ran a store. He ran a taxi service with his four-wheel-drive trucks, which he drove for fishermen, swimmers, and arriving and departing visitors to the island. He was his own man. I'm sure he would have been at home anywhere in the world, in his old cap with the broken visor shading his seamed, brown face, his eyes squinting, a pithy remark on his lips.

Big Jake was a good talker, but Little Jake is a cautious one with words. Tall and lean and slow to speak his mind is Little Jake. Some of the flavor went out of Ocracoke when they buried Big Jake, but Little Jake is still there to greet you with his slow smile.

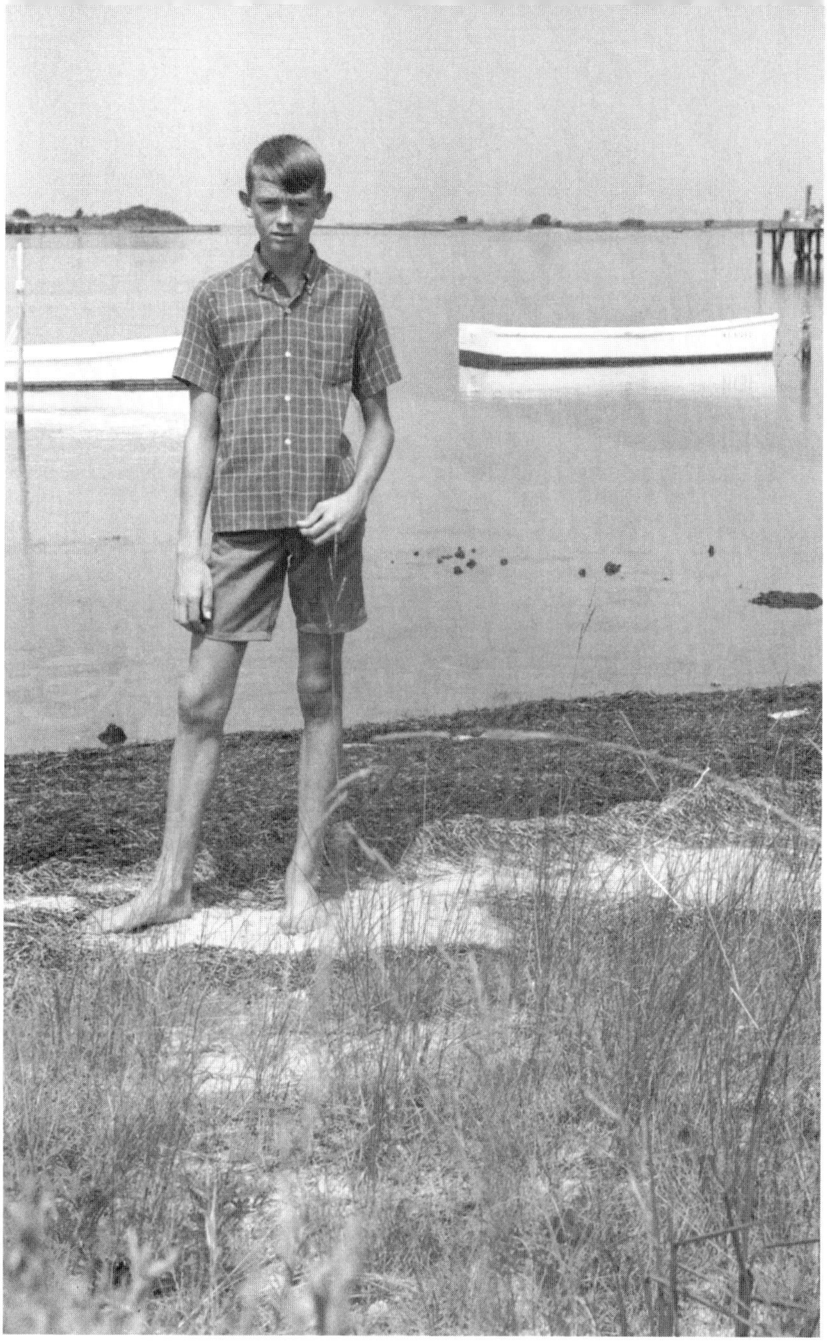

Kenny Ballance

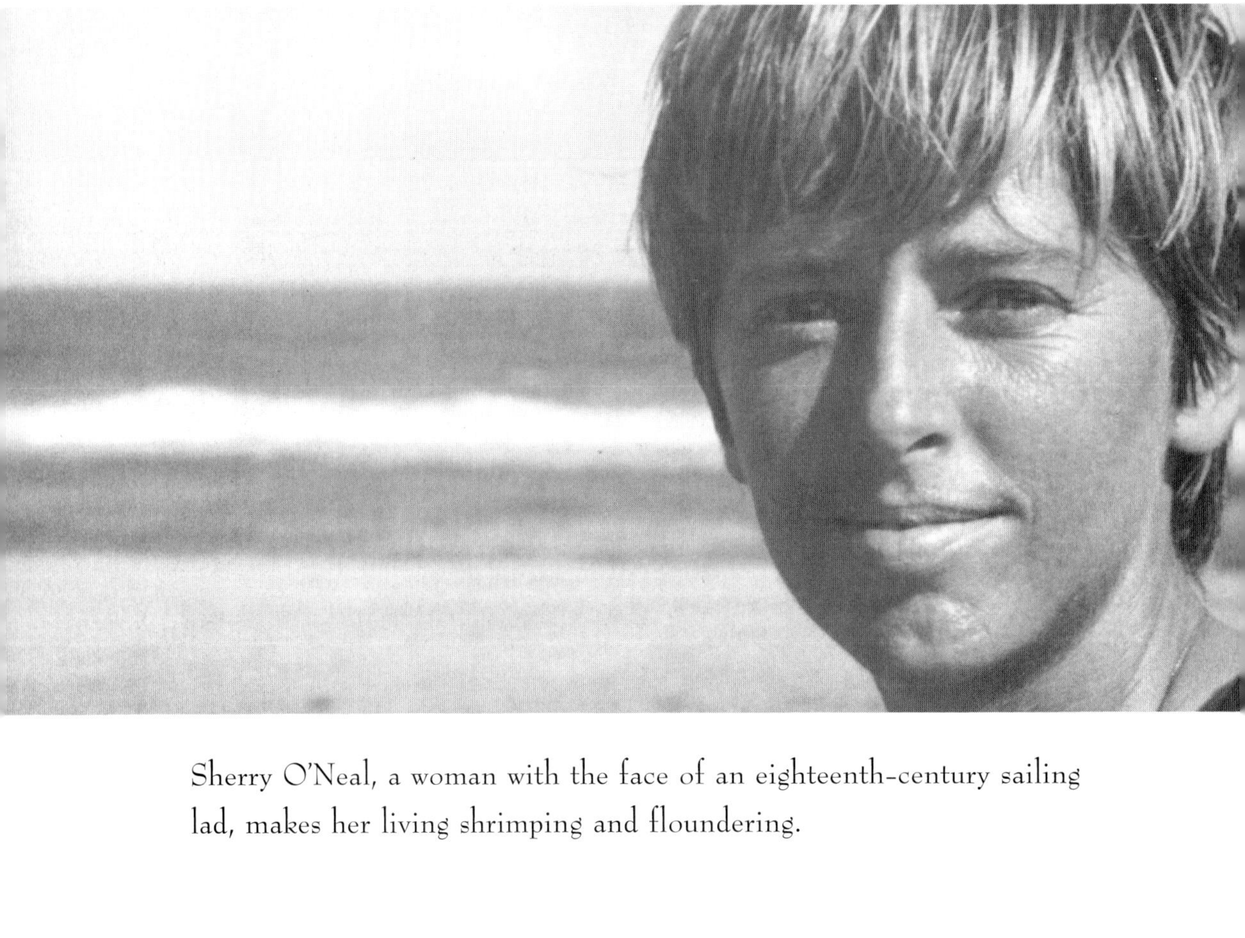

Sherry O'Neal, a woman with the face of an eighteenth-century sailing lad, makes her living shrimping and floundering.

Lucy O'Neal Gaskins and her son

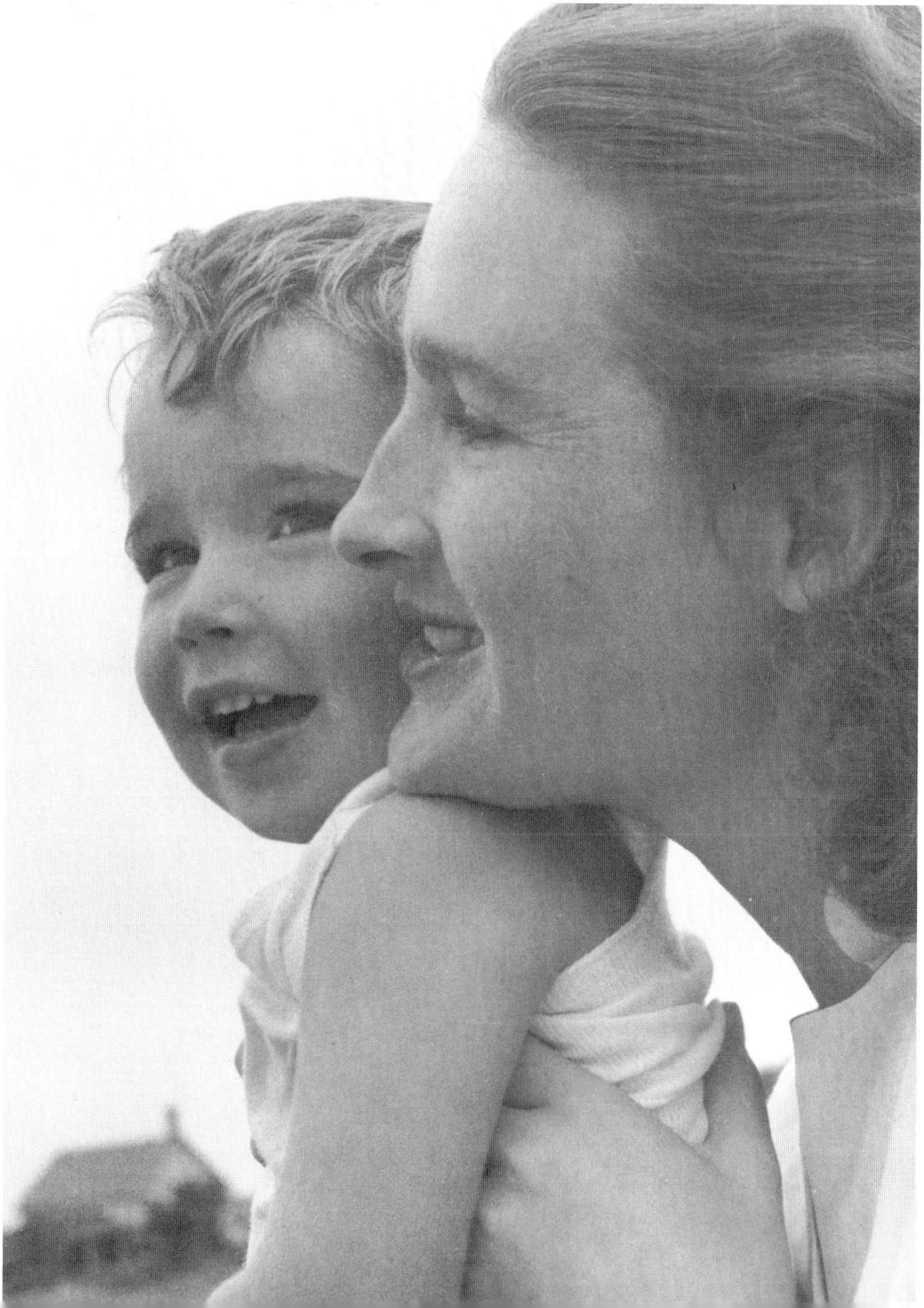

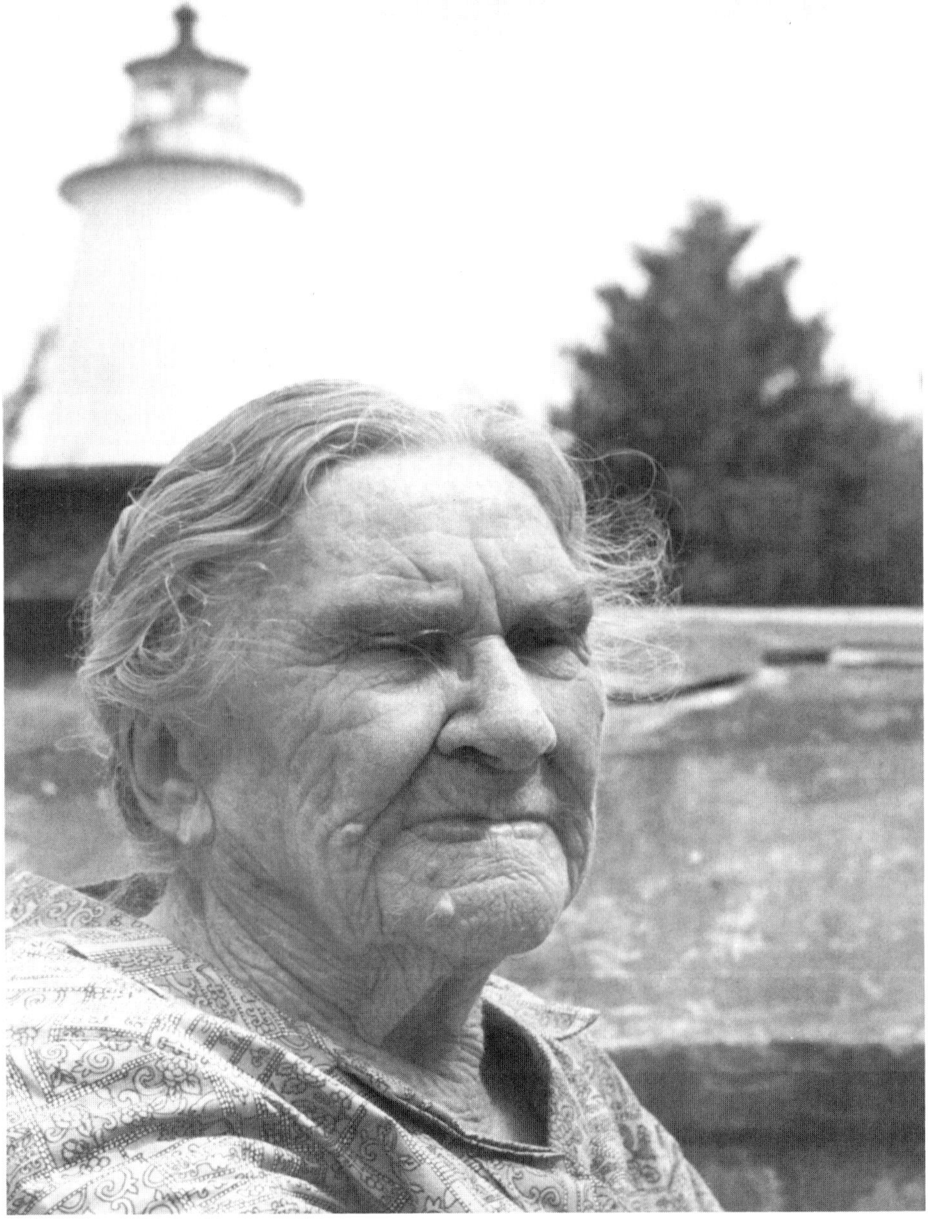

Mrs. Ben Gaskill, known as "Miss Sarah Ellen," has lived on Ocracoke all of her ninety years and raised five sons here.

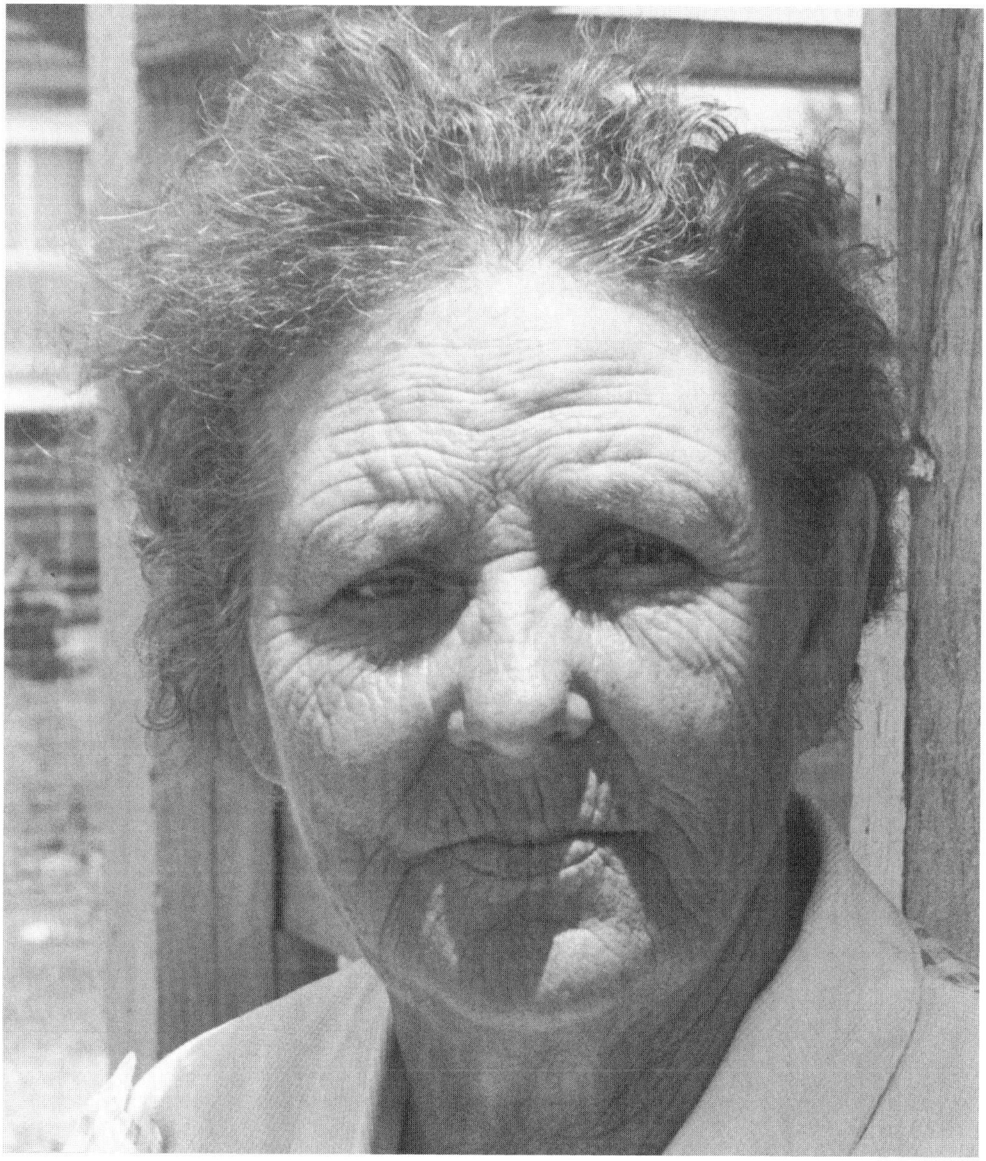

Miss Myra, Jake Alligood's wife, said, "All you need on Ocracoke is what you can put in a suitcase. Anything else you have, the sea will get it."

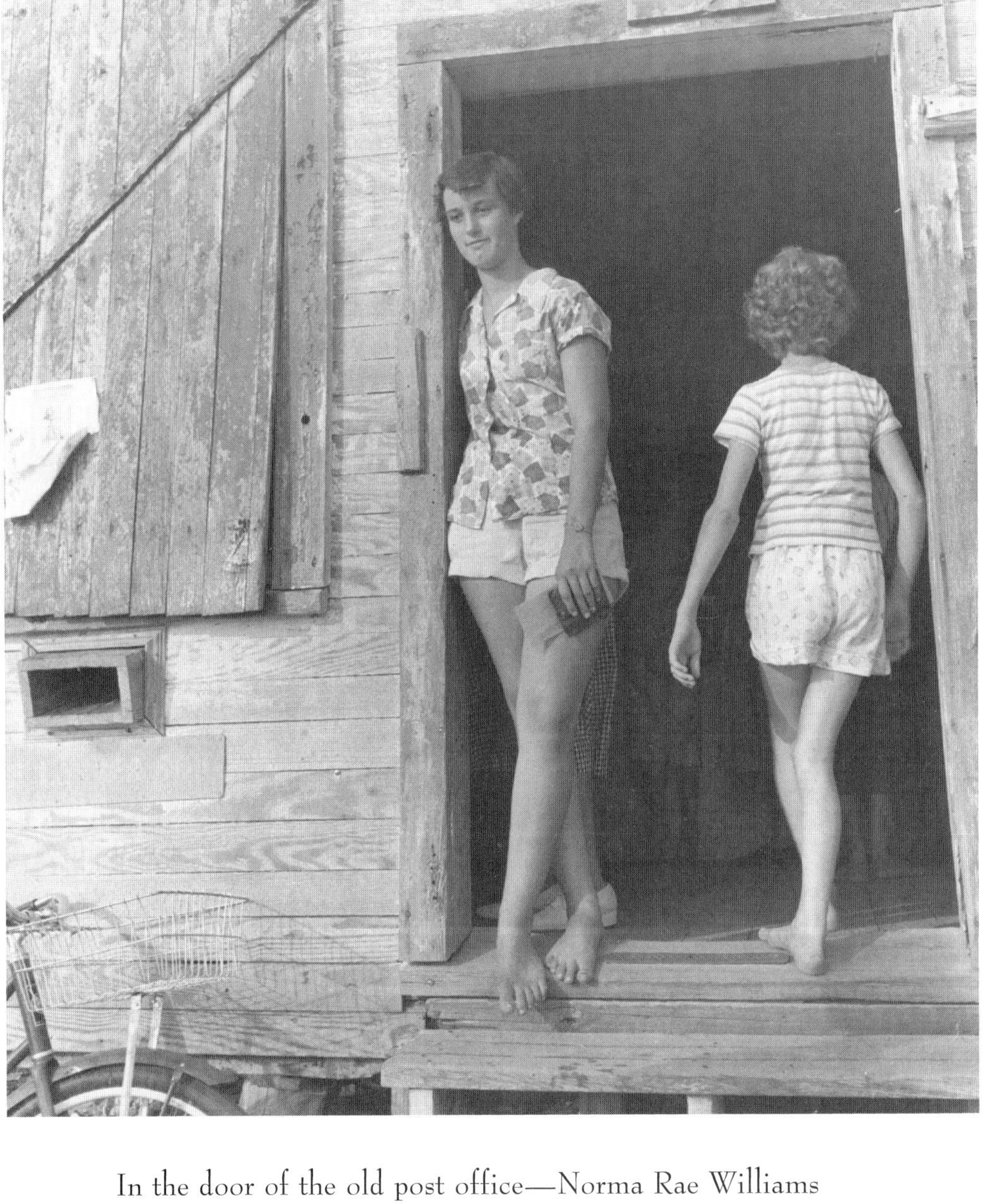

In the door of the old post office—Norma Rae Williams

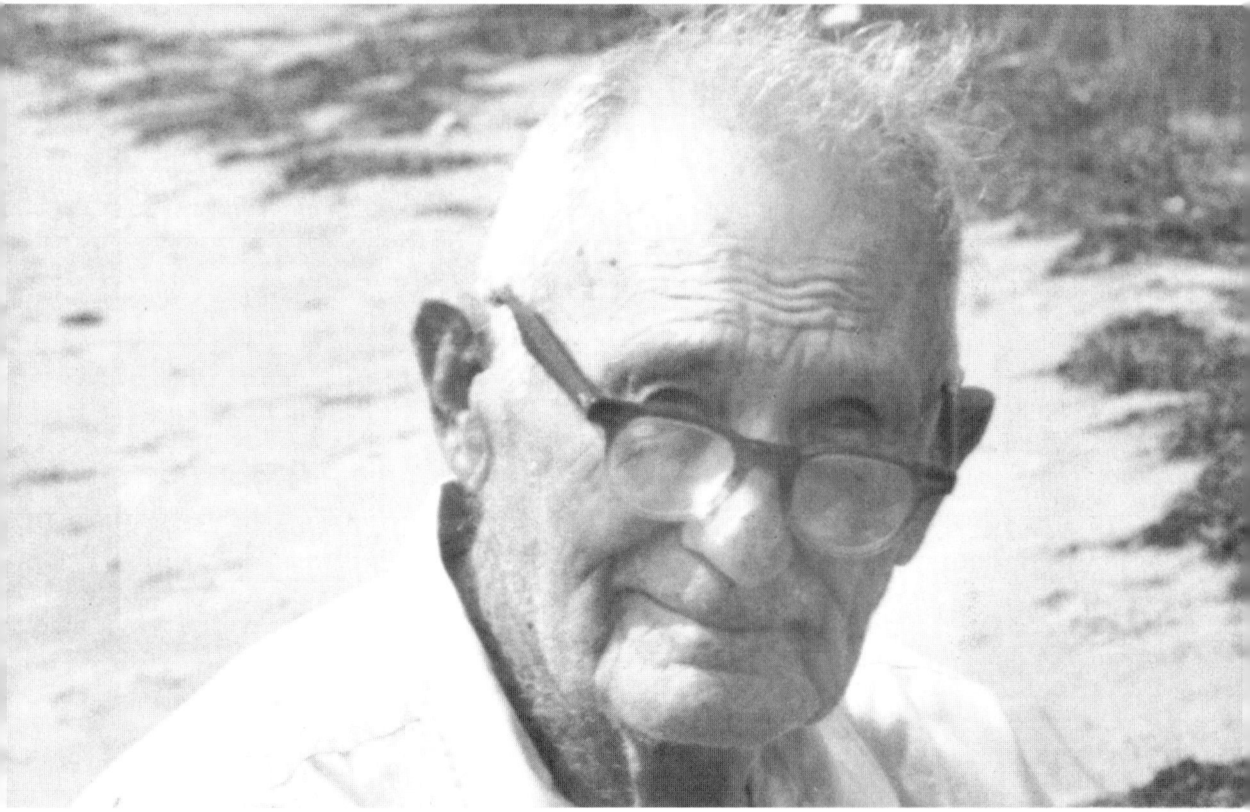

Mr. Tommie Howard, a charming ninety-two-year-old and the postmaster for many years, is known as a great storyteller.

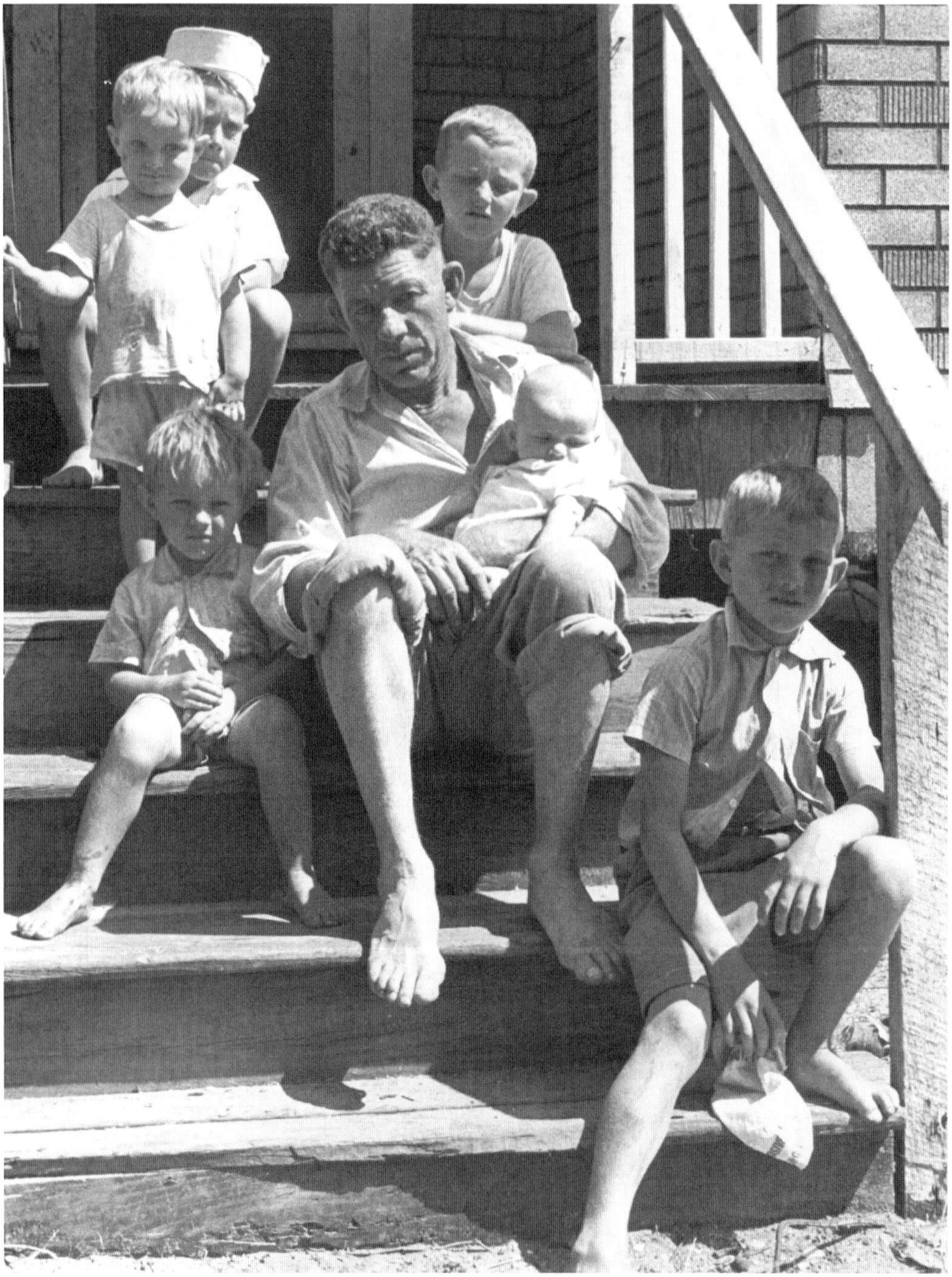

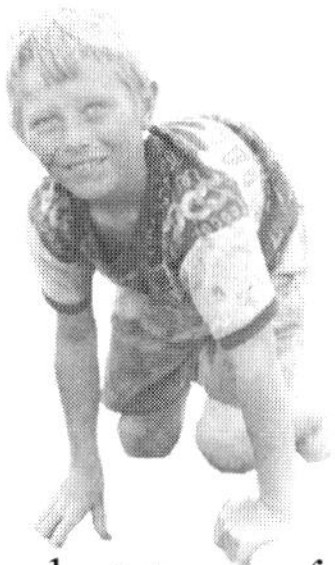

Three out of four Ocracoke boys grow up to join the Coast Guard, which began in 1874 as the Lifesaving Service. There were lots of lives to save, for those old days were tough ones, ships continuously coming to grief on the Banks. The men patrolled the beaches on foot and on horseback. Many of them could not swim, and it took a lot of courage to be willing to risk your own life helping to launch the twenty-six-hundred-pound lifeboats into the roaring surf. As the saying went, "The rules say you gotta go, not that you gotta come back."

The Coast Guard nowadays works with high-powered boats, helicopters, radio, and radar. Most wrecks are prevented, but there are plenty of other problems—boat trouble, fire, illness, airplanes nosed over, cars stuck, and tourists straying too far into the sea or getting lost. The Coast Guardsmen are there to help, too, when the hurricanes come. A gale warning at Hatteras can mean all kinds of damage. Winds of 110 miles per hour have been recorded, and one storm blew away the wind gauge.

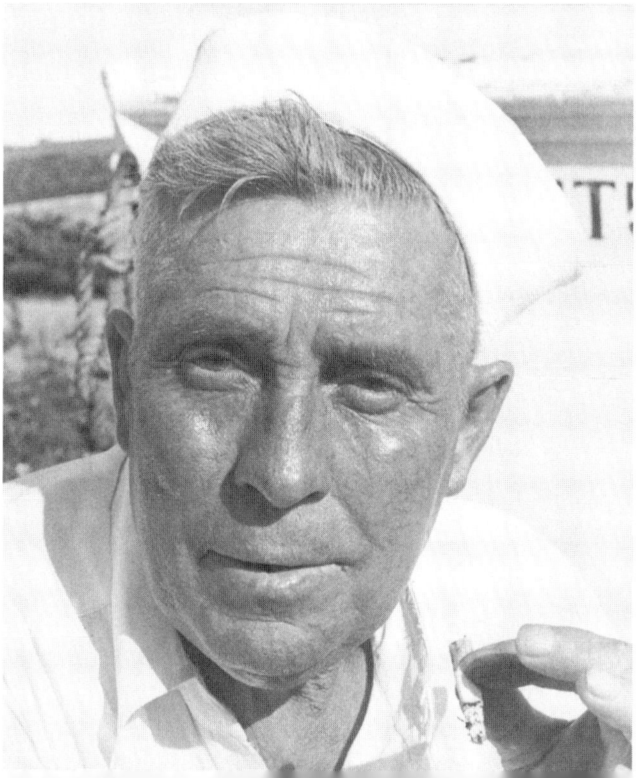

The three-story Coast Guard station guards the north side of the narrow entrance to Ocracoke Harbor.

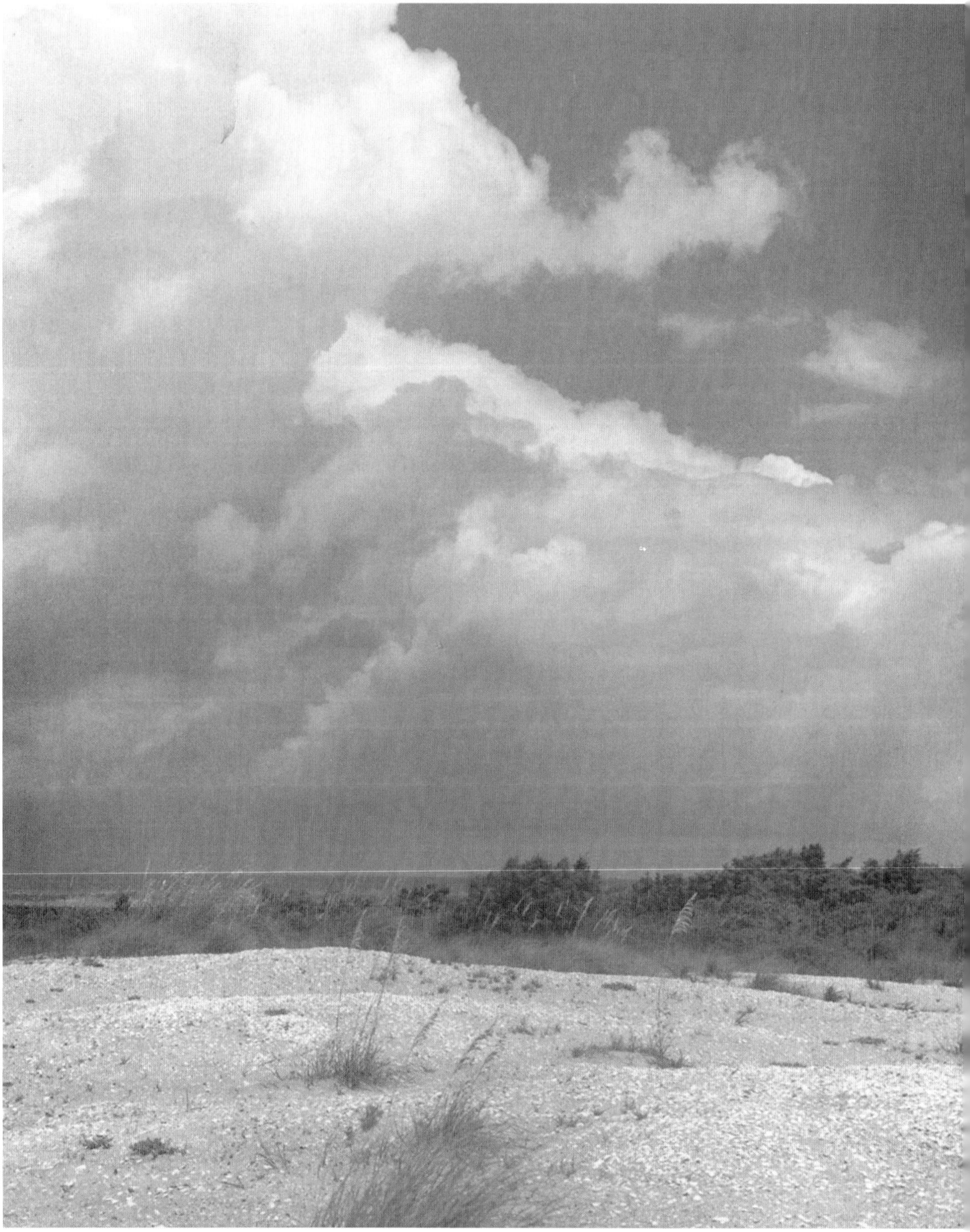

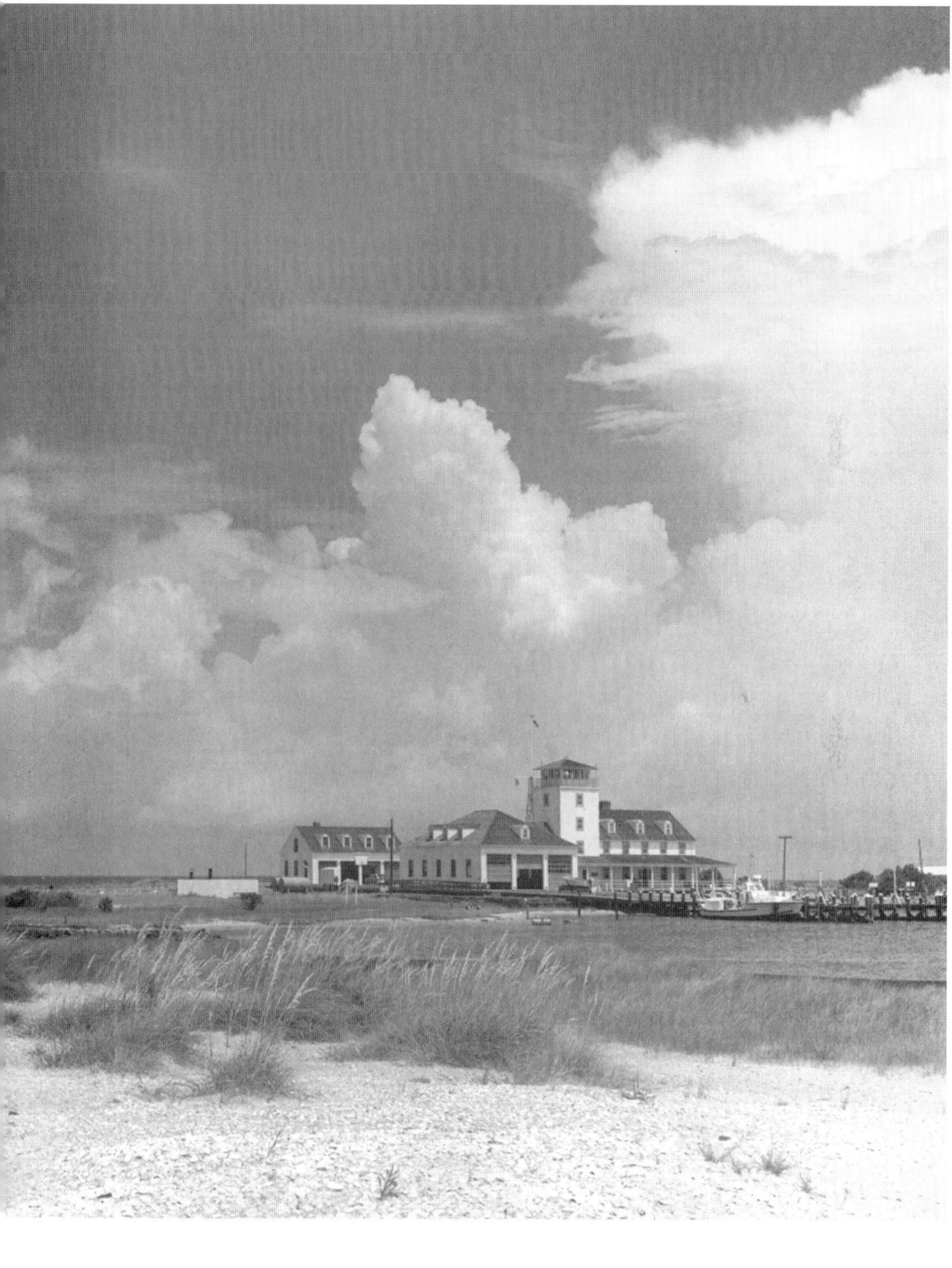

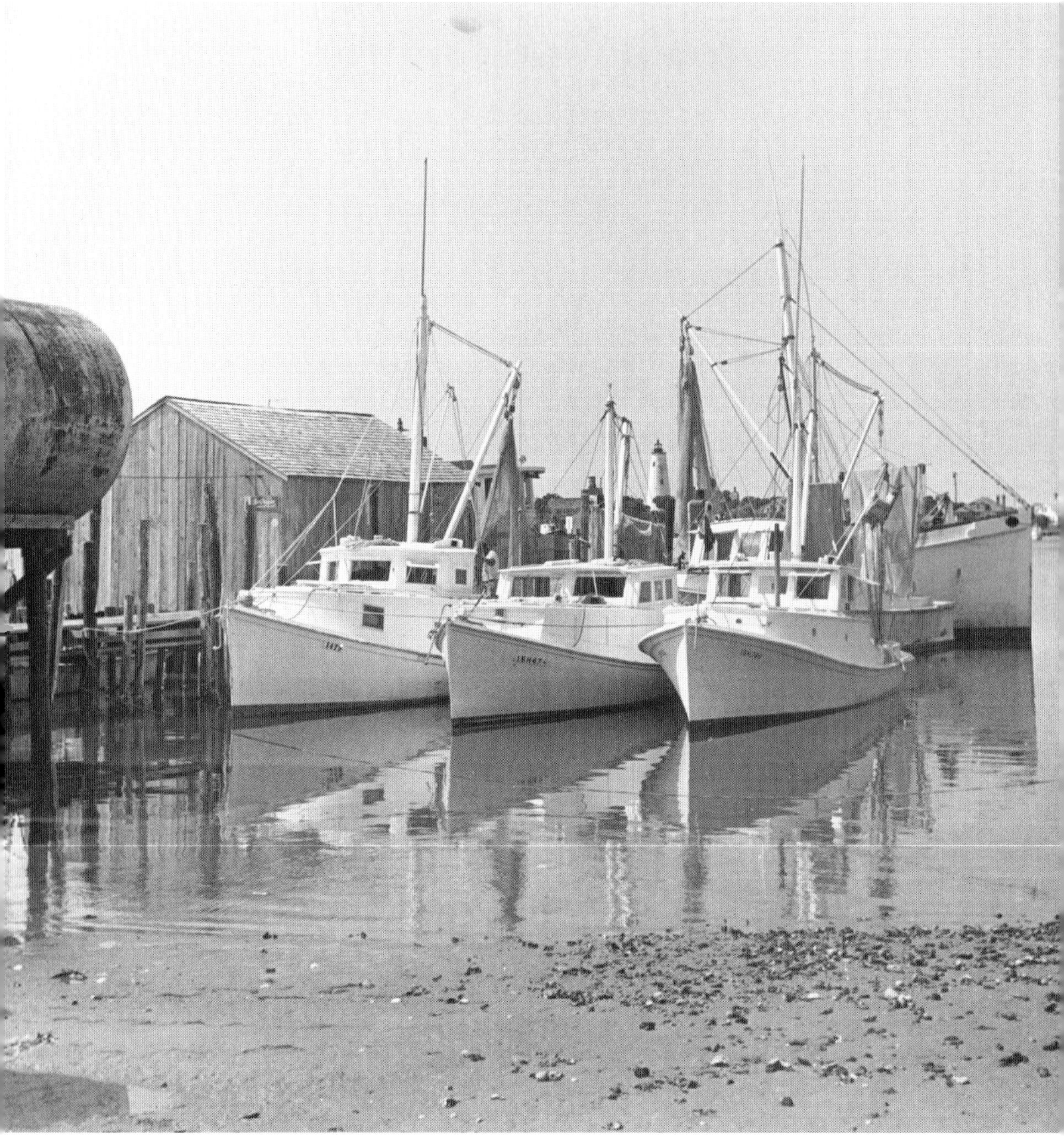

Ocracoke Harbor is also called Silver Lake. It used to be called Cookie Creek. It got its new name in 1923 when dredging turned it into an almost perfect circle of water that can accommodate quite large boats. To many islanders, it is still "the Creek."

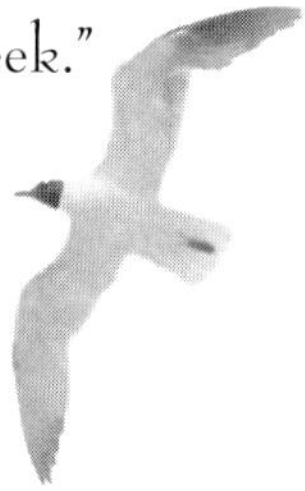

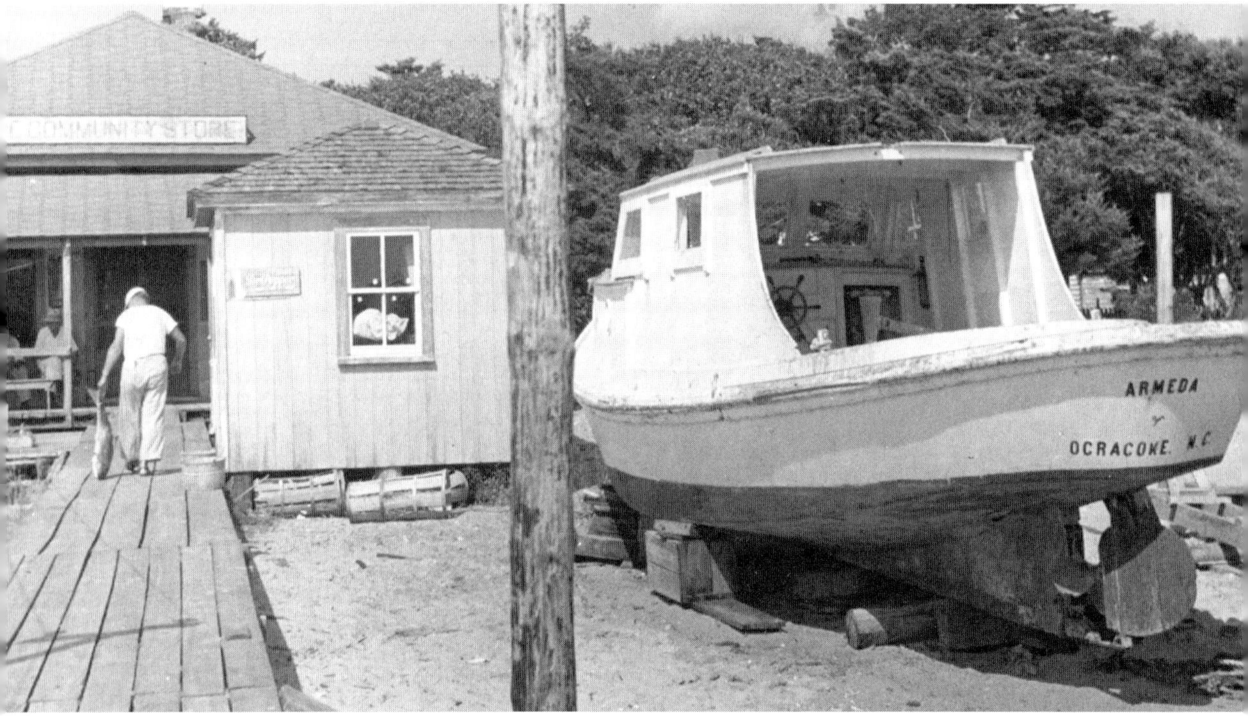

Shrimp boats, commercial fishing boats, charter boats, visiting yachts, and rowboats all tie up at the dock near the icehouse and the electric-light plant. Stores and the post office make this the business and shopping center of Ocracoke.

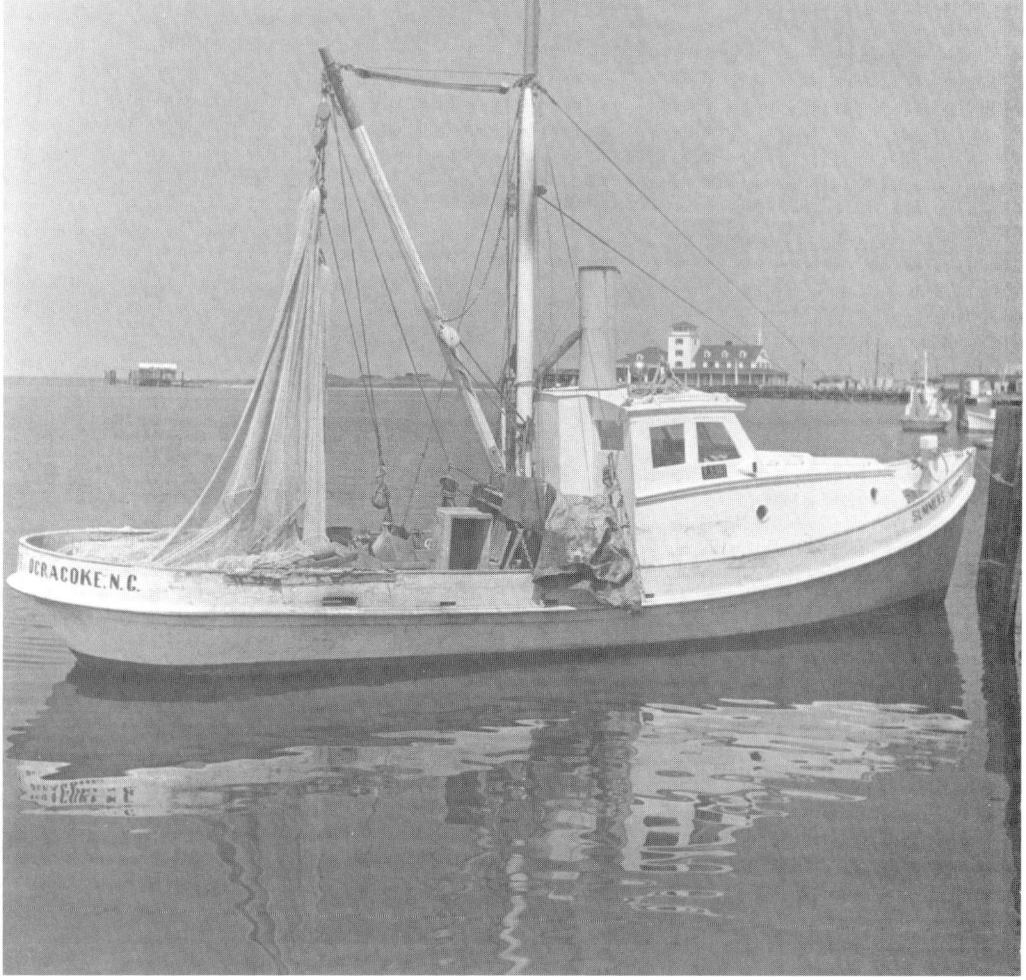
OCRACOKE, N.C.

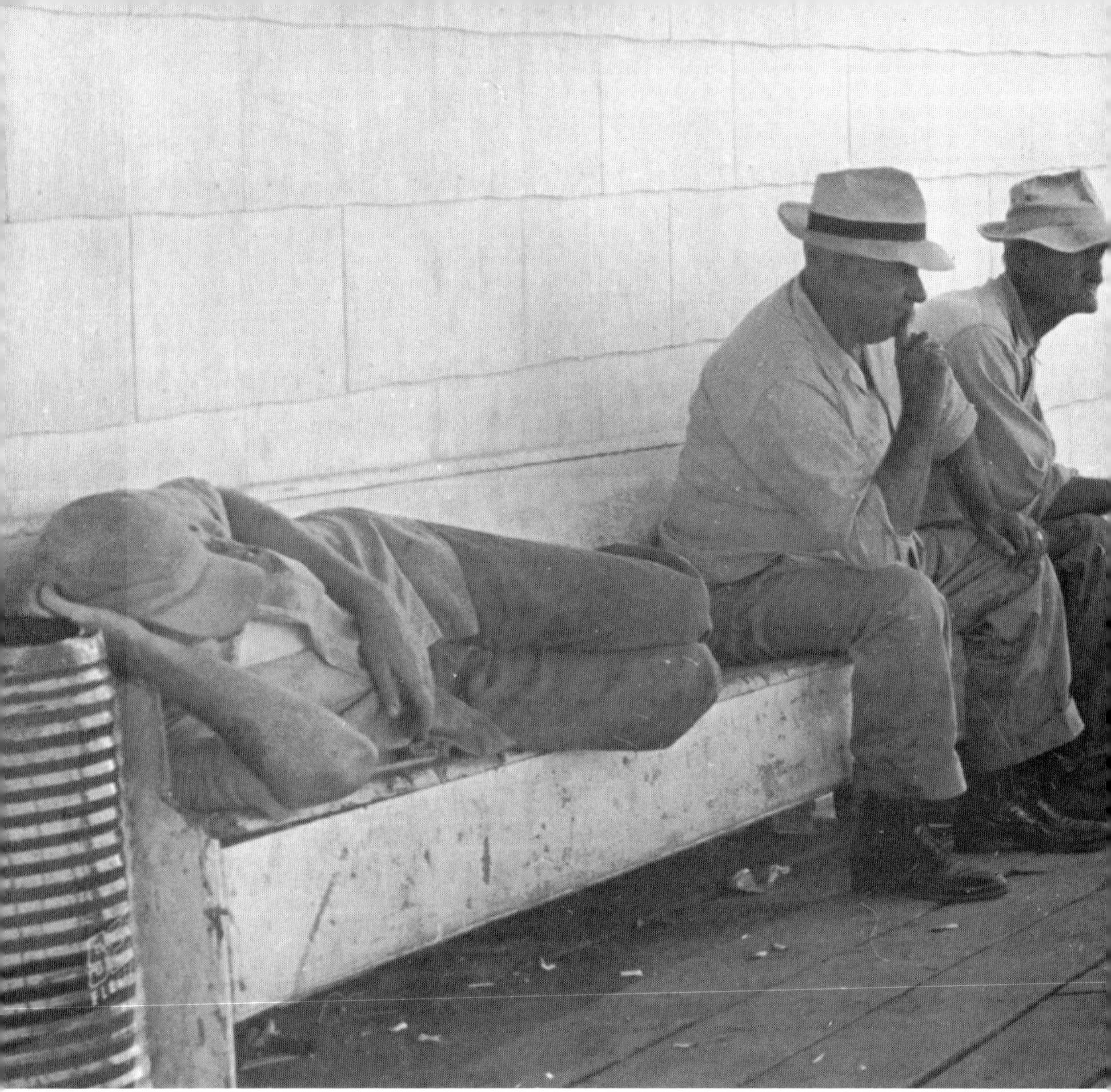

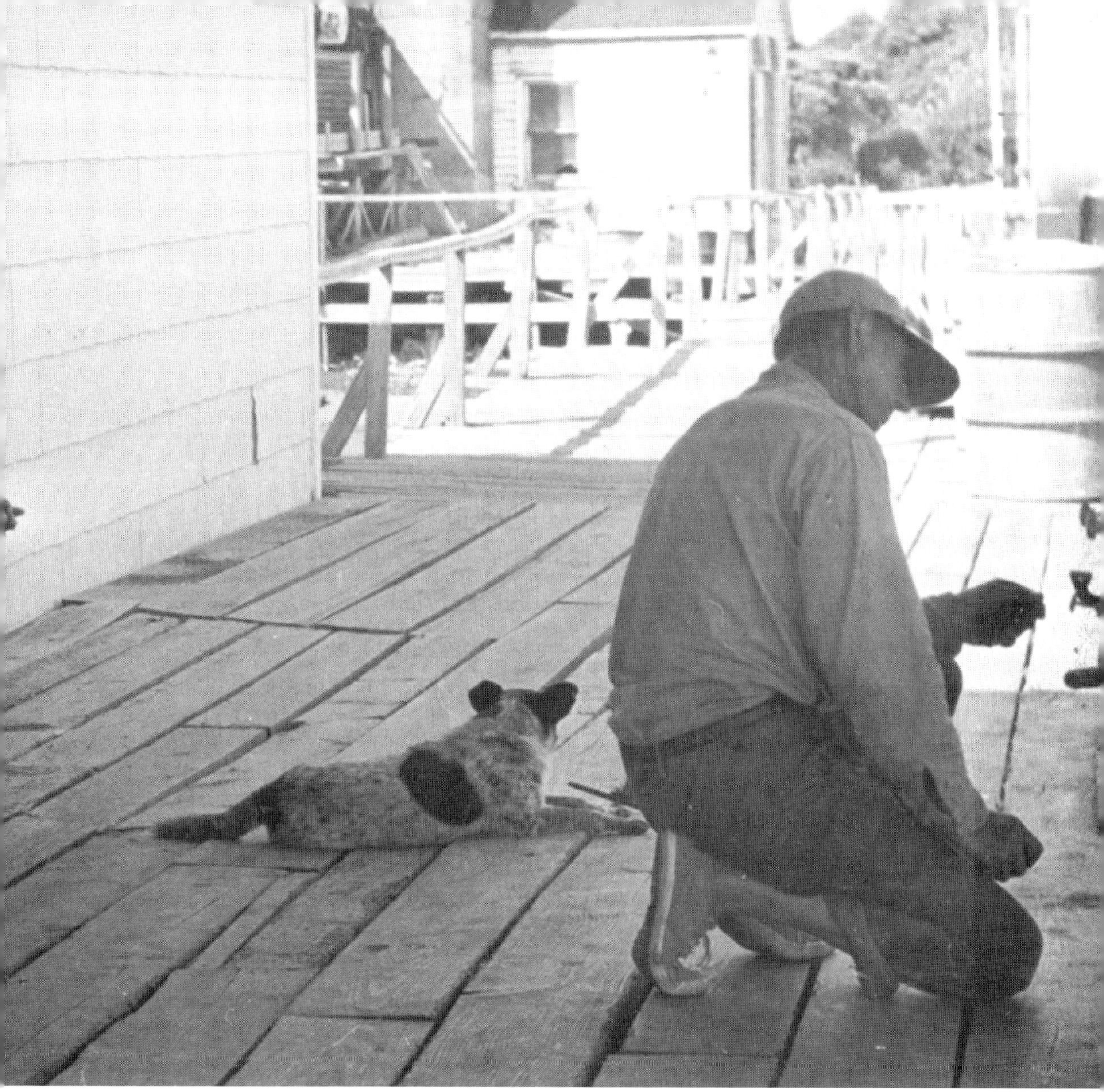

Sometimes, there is lots of activity around the docks. Sometimes, people just sit and think about fishing. All of the calm and the leisure that anyone could want is here.

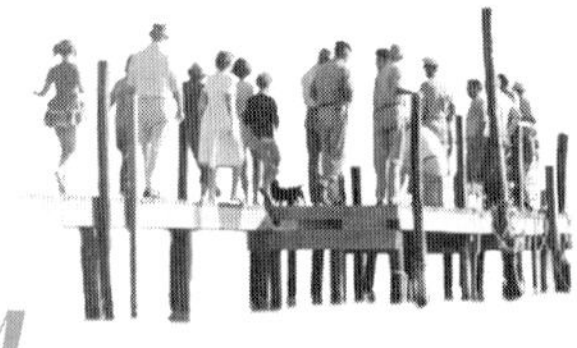

You choose your own pace. Of course, getting ready to fish can be very serious business when a lady is watching.

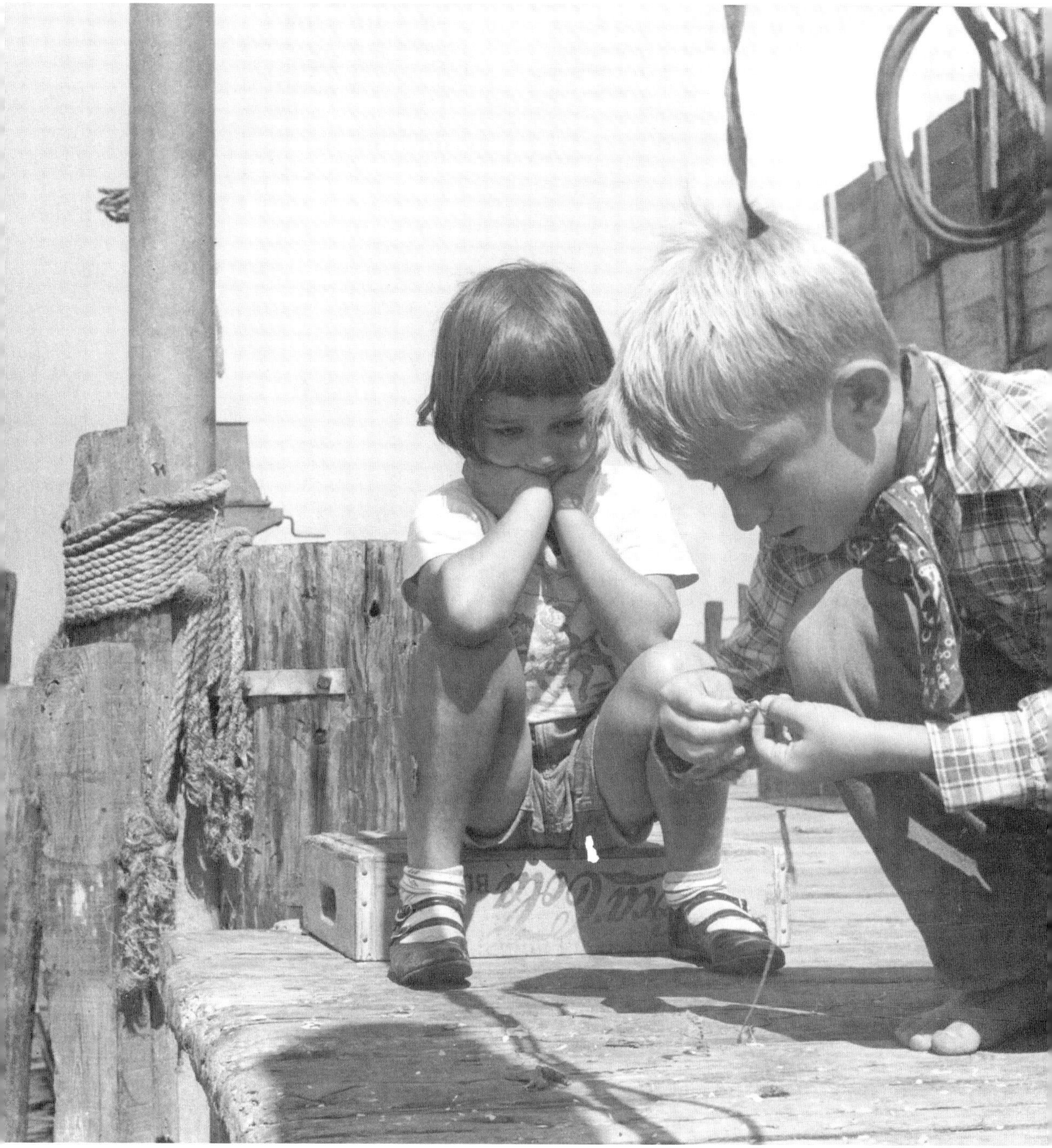

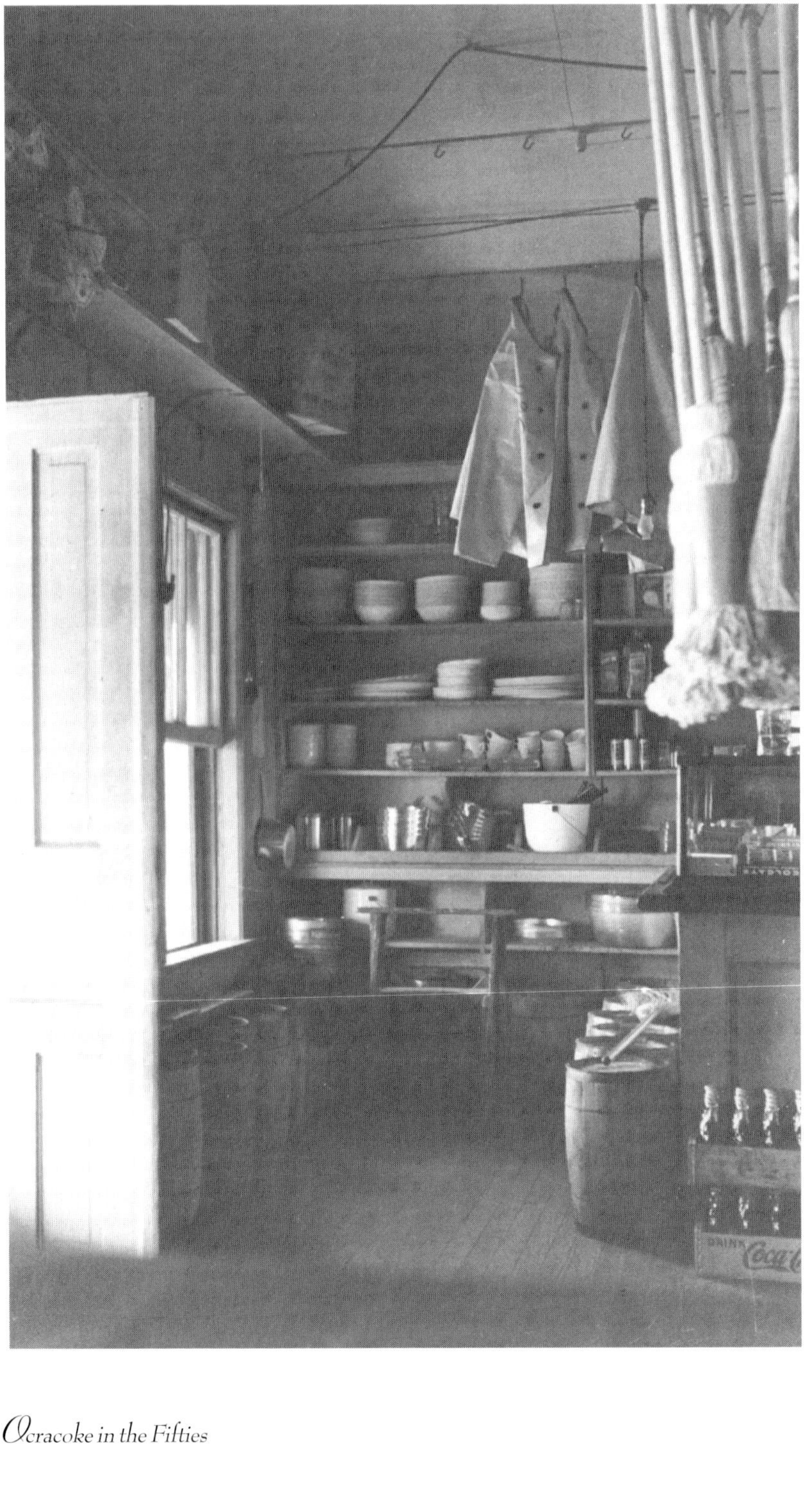

Coca-Co

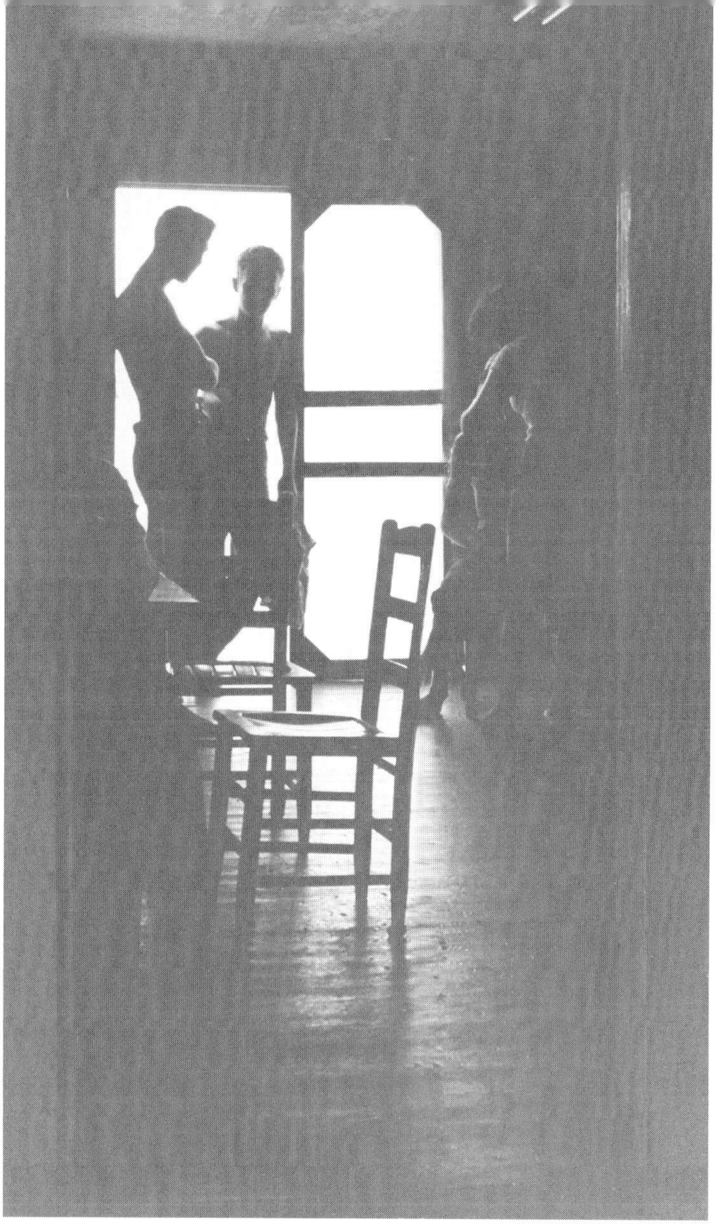

The stores carry food and some clothing. Meat used to come in just twice a week, and serious shopping required a trip to the mainland. Teenagers gathered for Cokes and ice cream. Ocracoke had no juvenile-delinquency problems.

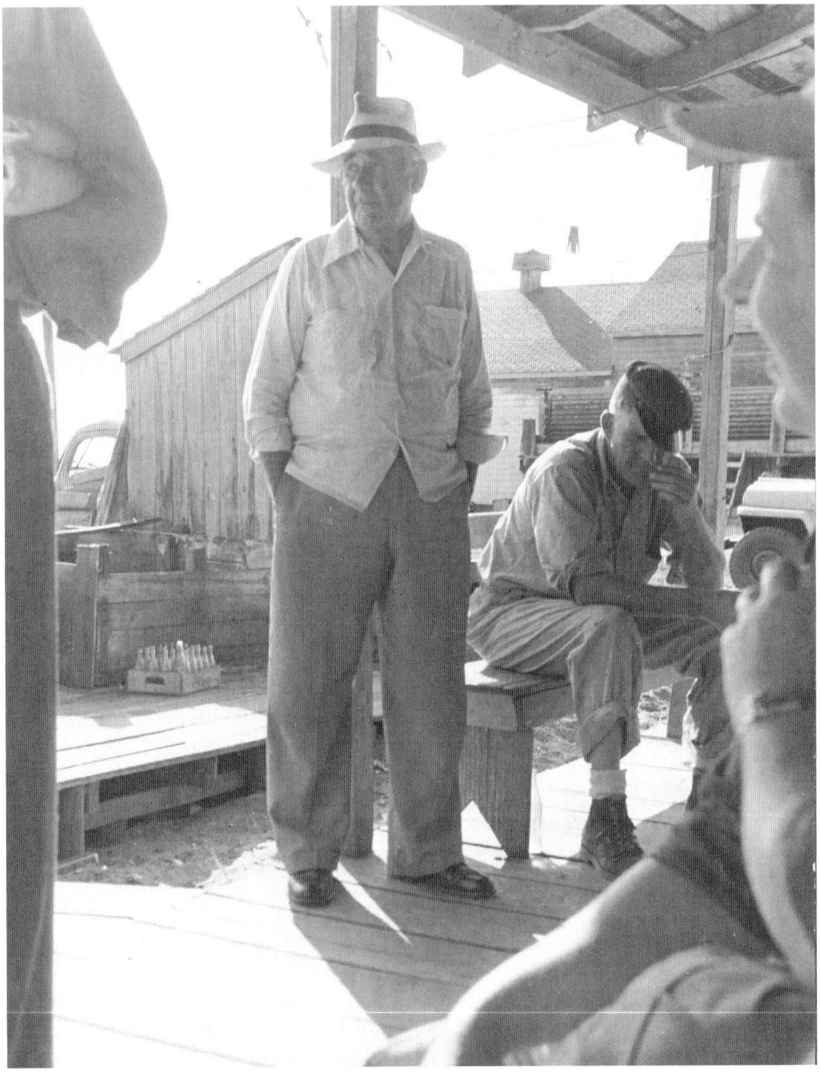

Around four-thirty, when the mailboat was due, the stores and docks came to life. People afoot, people in trucks and Jeeps—everyone who was free—gathered for the social hour of the day. Even the ponies would be there, standing in the shallow water swishing flies.

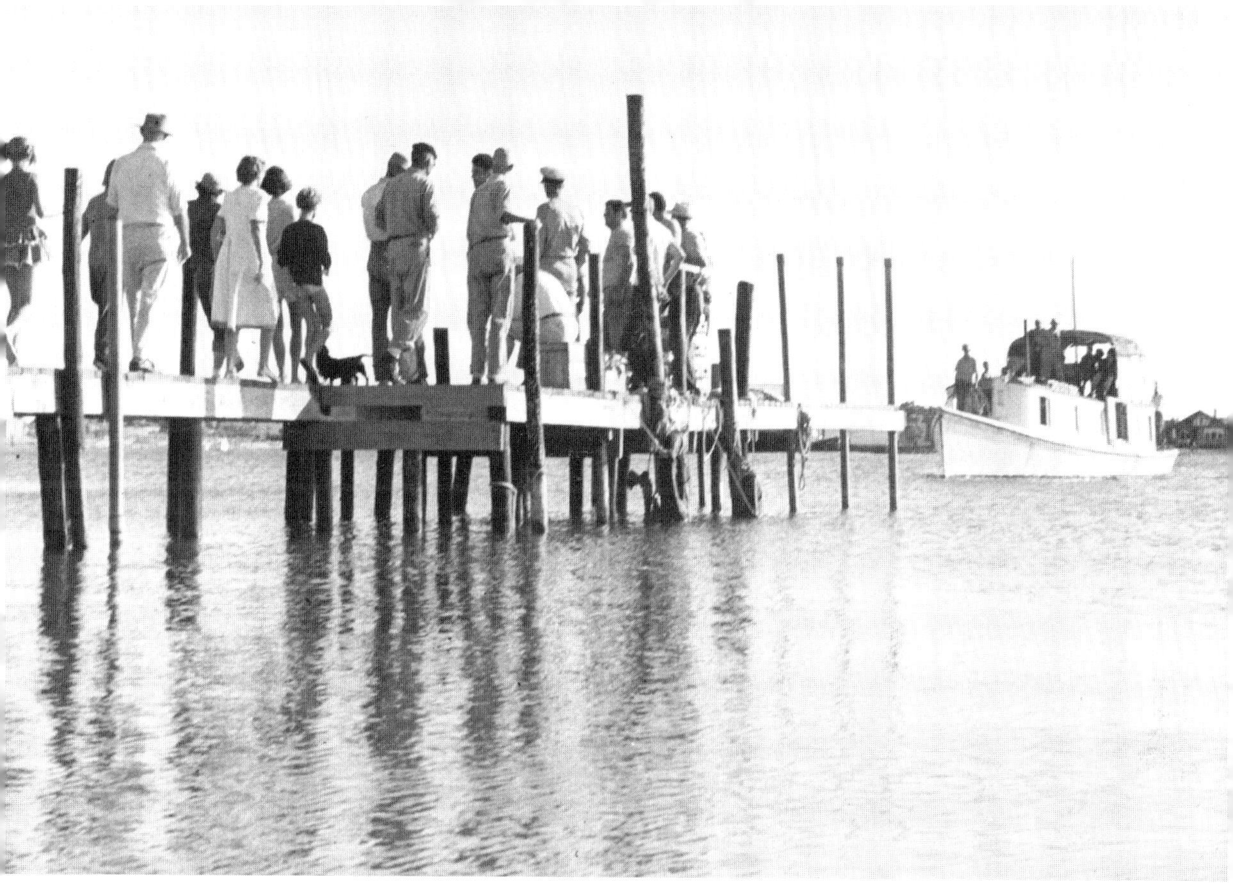

There was talk and gossip as to whether or not the mailboat would be on time. Islanders caught up on the events of the day while everyone waited for the mail, groceries, newspapers, friends returning home, and whatever strangers would turn up.

You got a quiet, friendly looking-over from the assembled islanders when you stepped off the boat after the four-hour trip from the town of Atlantic on the Carolina coast. The boat was not the ultimate in luxury. You might get a seat on a wooden bench or have to sit on some of the freight. You might be burned by the sun or soaked by the rain, but it never seemed to spoil the trip. Then the post office closed while the mail was sorted.

POST OFFICE

The Ocracoke post office, established in 1849, was the first on the Banks. The original postmaster was William Howard. For years, the modern postmaster was Tom Howard. Today, the postmaster in the red-brick building is dark-haired Mrs. Elizabeth Howard.

There is a lot of continuity on Ocracoke. In times past, it didn't take long to sort the mail. The people chatted while they waited, the children played along the shore, the ponies ambled off. Then the post-office door opened again. There was a final swirl of activity before everyone drifted home to Ocracoke's early supper.

There were other ways to reach Ocracoke besides the mailboat. You could ride the mail bus down the Banks, crossing from Hatteras by ferry. It was a jolting, backbreaking trip down the island's almost nonexistent road, and you shared the bus with the mail, the freight, and even livestock.

You could drive the beach yourself if the tide was low and you were lucky.

You could fly in if you didn't care how small the plane was, or that the only place to land was the beach. Pilots who knew the Banks could tell by the color of the sand where to come down safely. Hit a soft spot and you'd nose over. In the old days, expected or not, you just waited beside the plane until a truck or Jeep

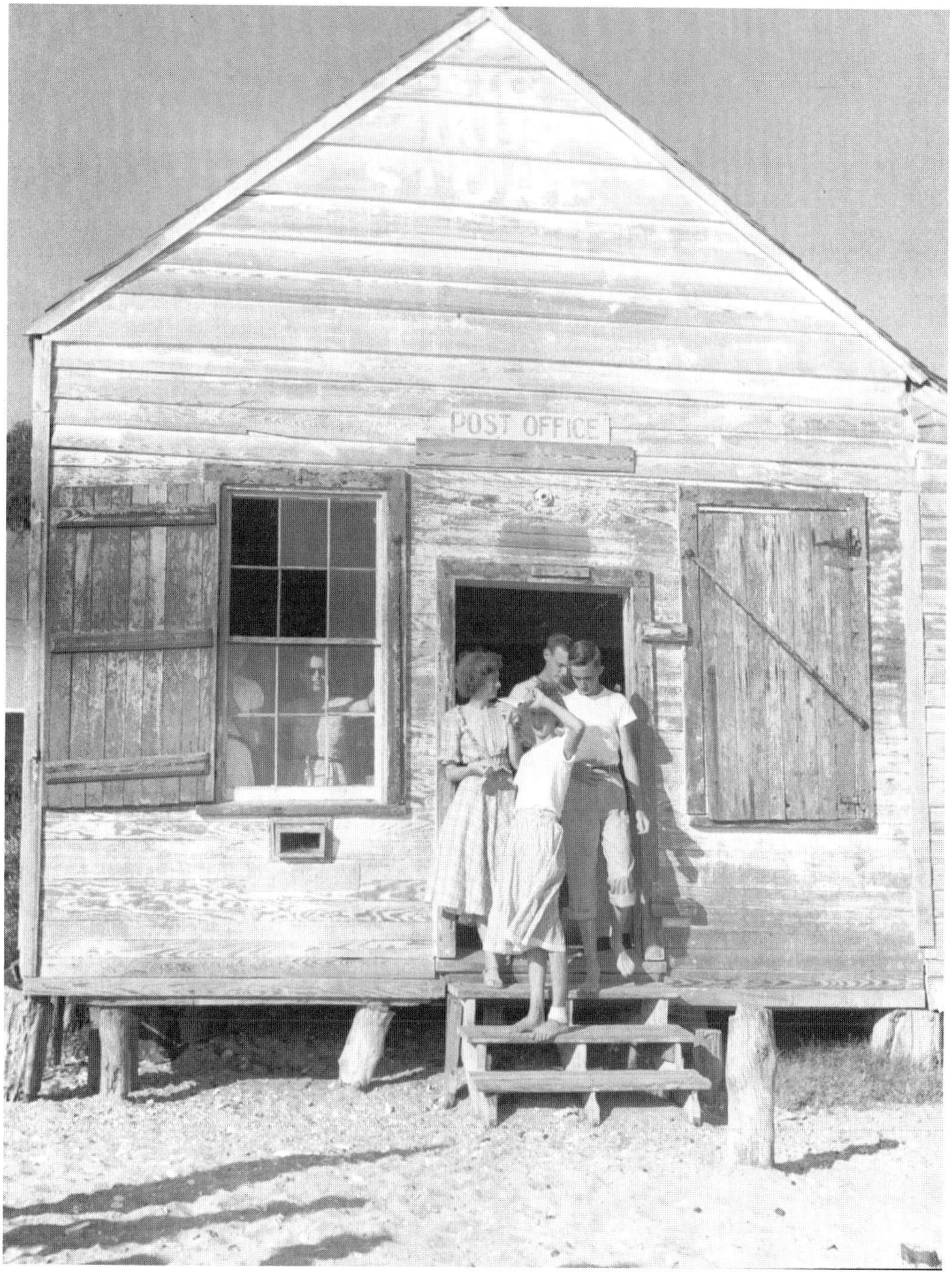
POST OFFICE

turned up. The driver would lean out to casually inquire, "Where you want me to carry you?"

Now, you can drive an ordinary car all the way to Ocracoke village on a surfaced road. The state-operated Hatteras ferry runs on a regular schedule. The ferry from Silver Lake to Cedar Island that goes and comes twice a day carries thirty-seven cars and looks as big as the *Queen Elizabeth*.

And there is a new cement airstrip, where cars meet you and carry you off to an air-conditioned motel with television.

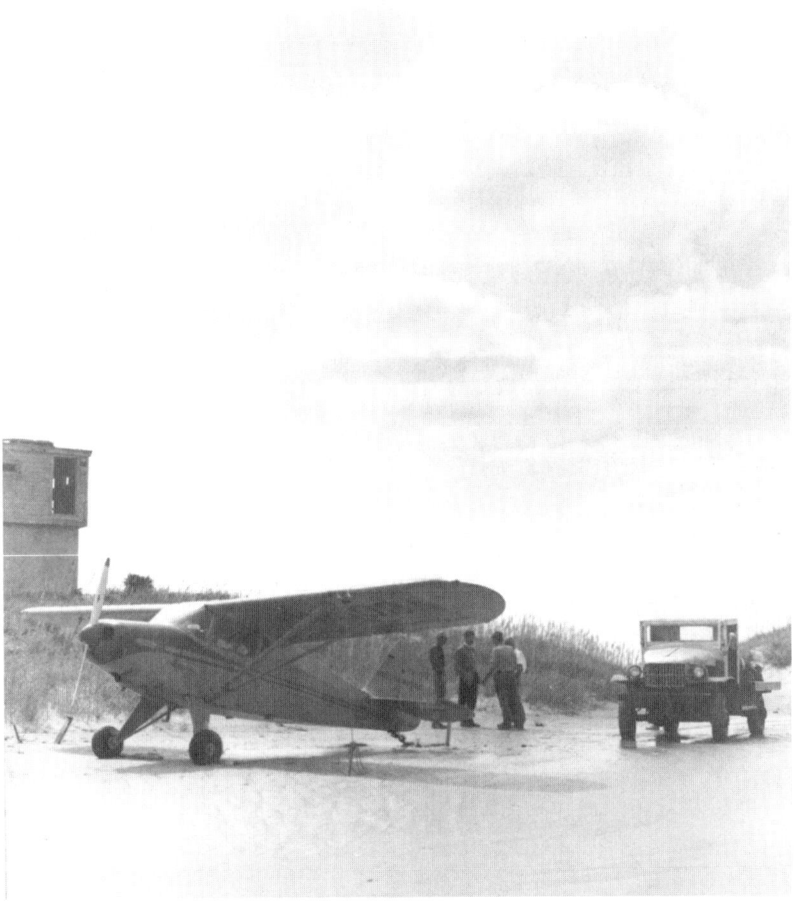

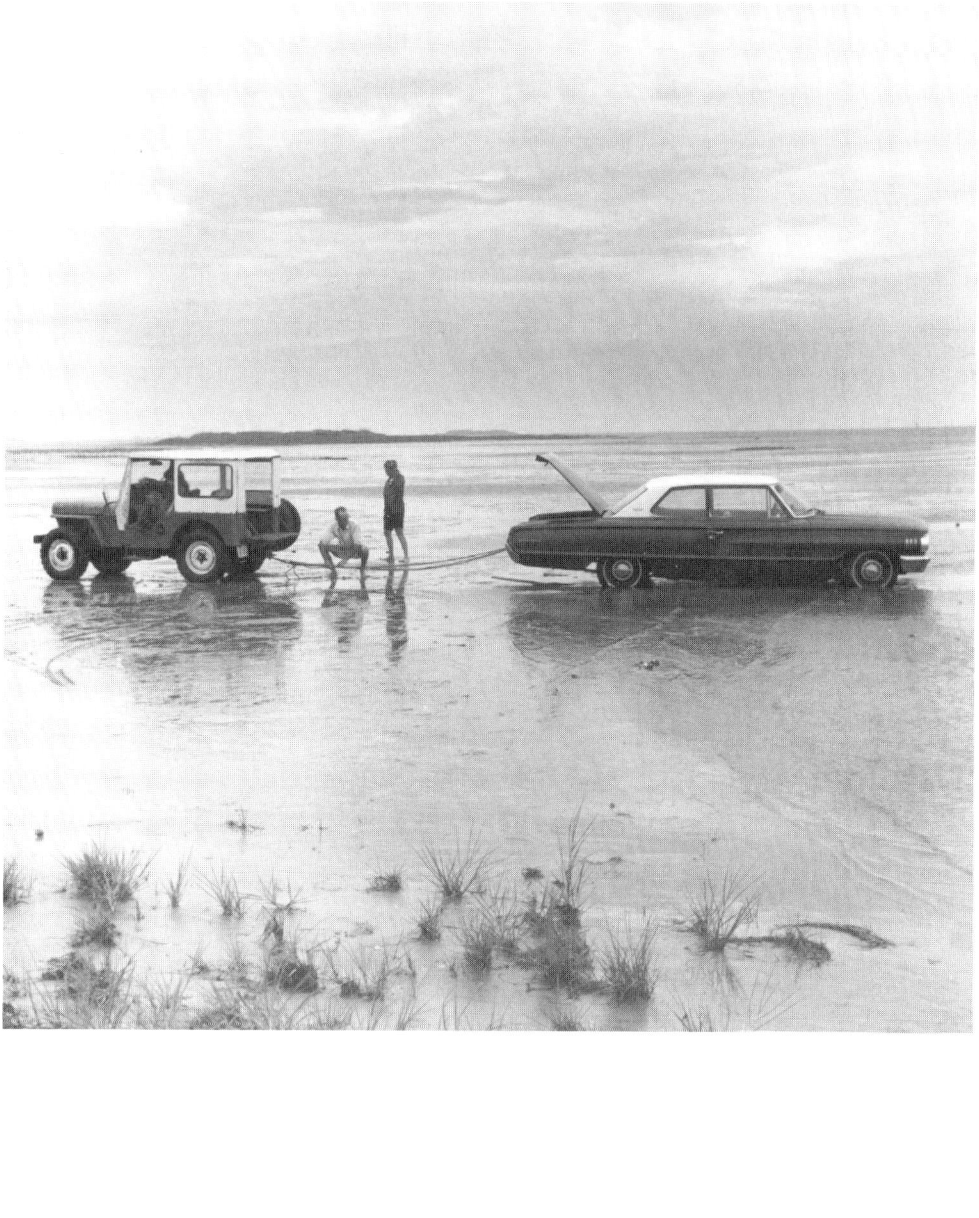

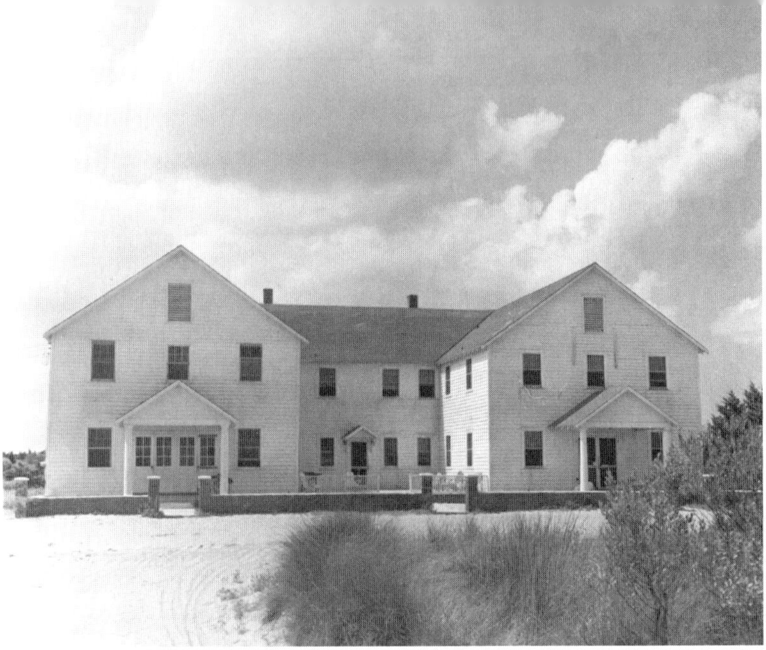

Once, you might have been taken to the Wahab Village Hotel, simple, informal, and comfortable. There was plenty of plain food, a movie once a week, and no need to put on a pair of shoes from the moment you arrived until you reluctantly left.

Your host was C. F. Boyette, former Latin teacher, former physical-education instructor, an easygoing man with a delightful sense of humor. The hotel was on the beach but not on the sea. From an upstairs window, you could just glimpse the water like a ruler line on the horizon.

Newcomers might say, "We thought the hotel was up the beach."

"It is," said Mr. Boyette.

"But where's the ocean? We wanted a swim."

"Right over there about a mile and a quarter. You could walk."

"Walk?" they might ask.

"Or I could get Jake to carry you across."

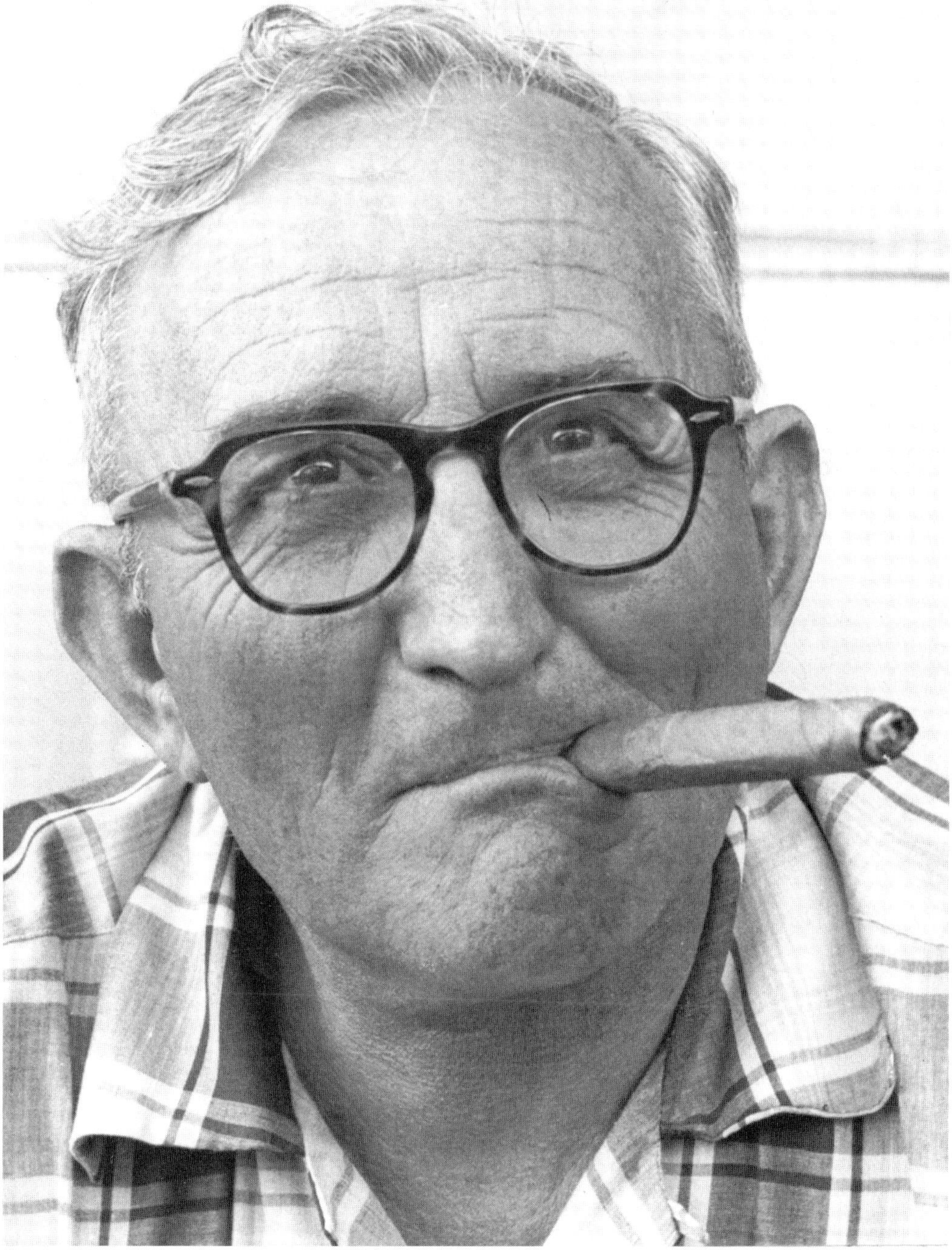

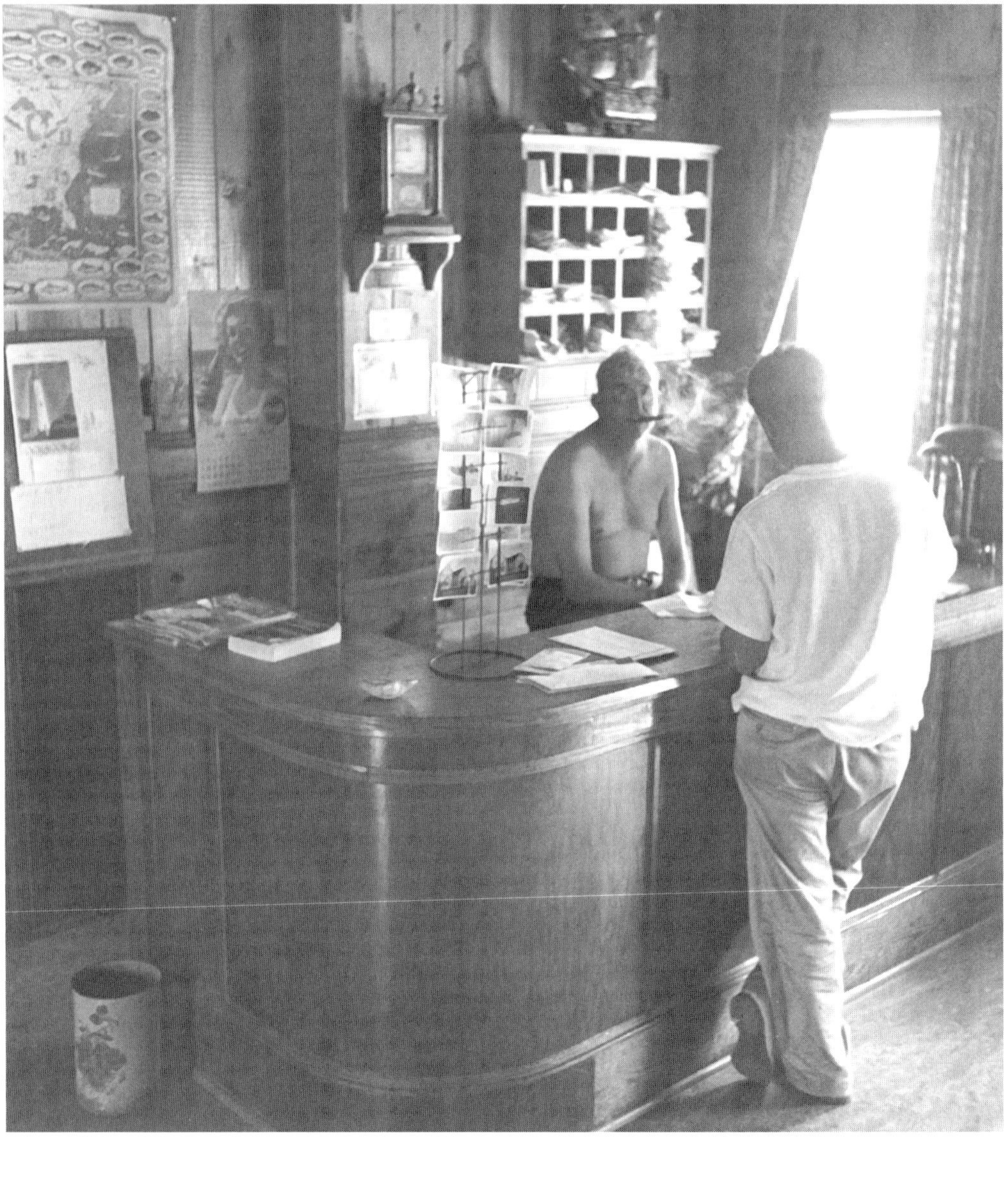

A **party** of people just off a plane would ask, "What can we do for entertainment?"

"Might walk down and look at the docks. Don't know if it'd entertain you," Mr. Boyette would answer.

"What about nightlife?"

"Movie every Saturday," Mr. Boyette replied.

Ocracoke is not for people looking for entertainment or nightlife, but there is plenty to do if you want. On the beach, on a good day, you can fill a bucket with crabs in no time. You can go floundering by night in the shallow water of the sound, a lantern in one hand and a rough spear in the other. The running tide and small fish push against your legs. Seabirds, disturbed by the light, flash white against a black velvet sky.

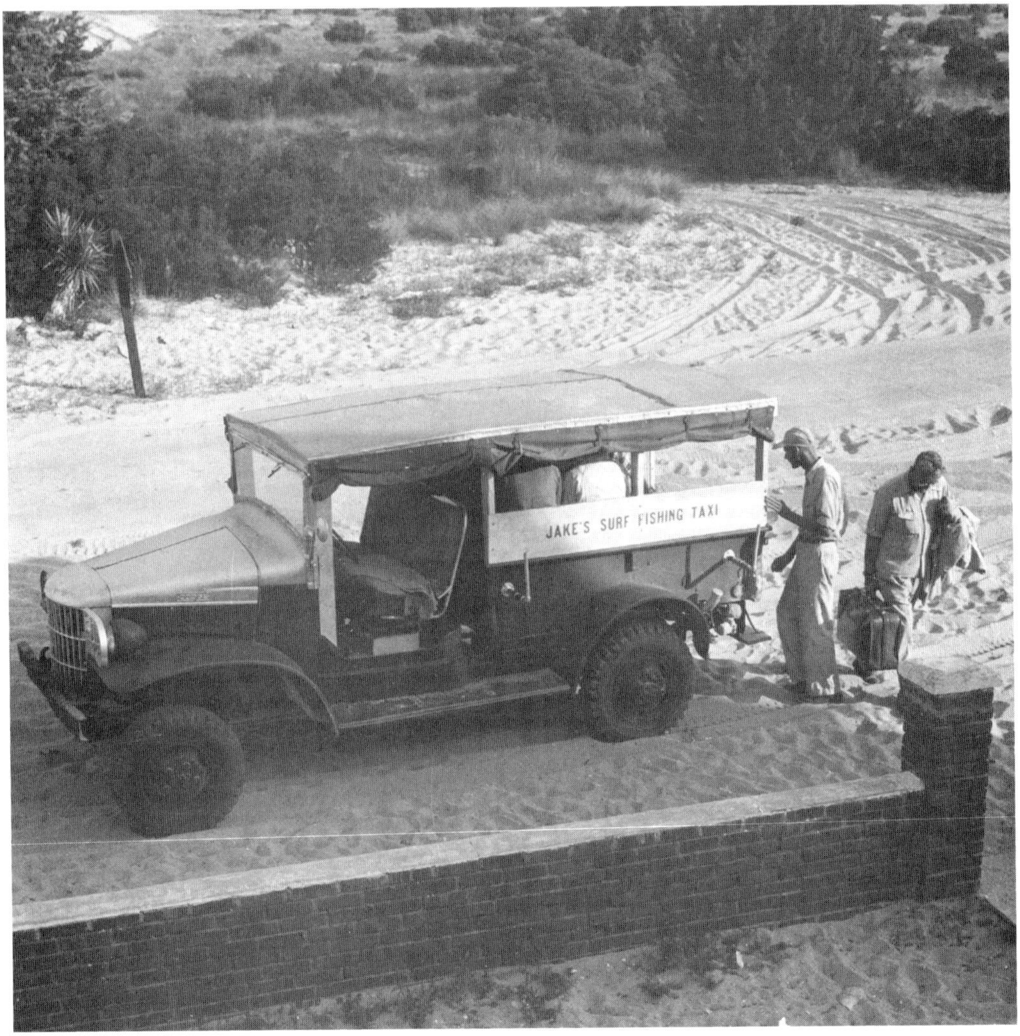
JAKE'S SURF FISHING TAXI

Jake's taxi would take you where you wanted to go, but the way to absorb the island's atmosphere was to walk with the sand hot under your feet. You might start perhaps at Silver Lake and follow the shoreline of the sound, where you'd see the patterns made by the fishing nets.

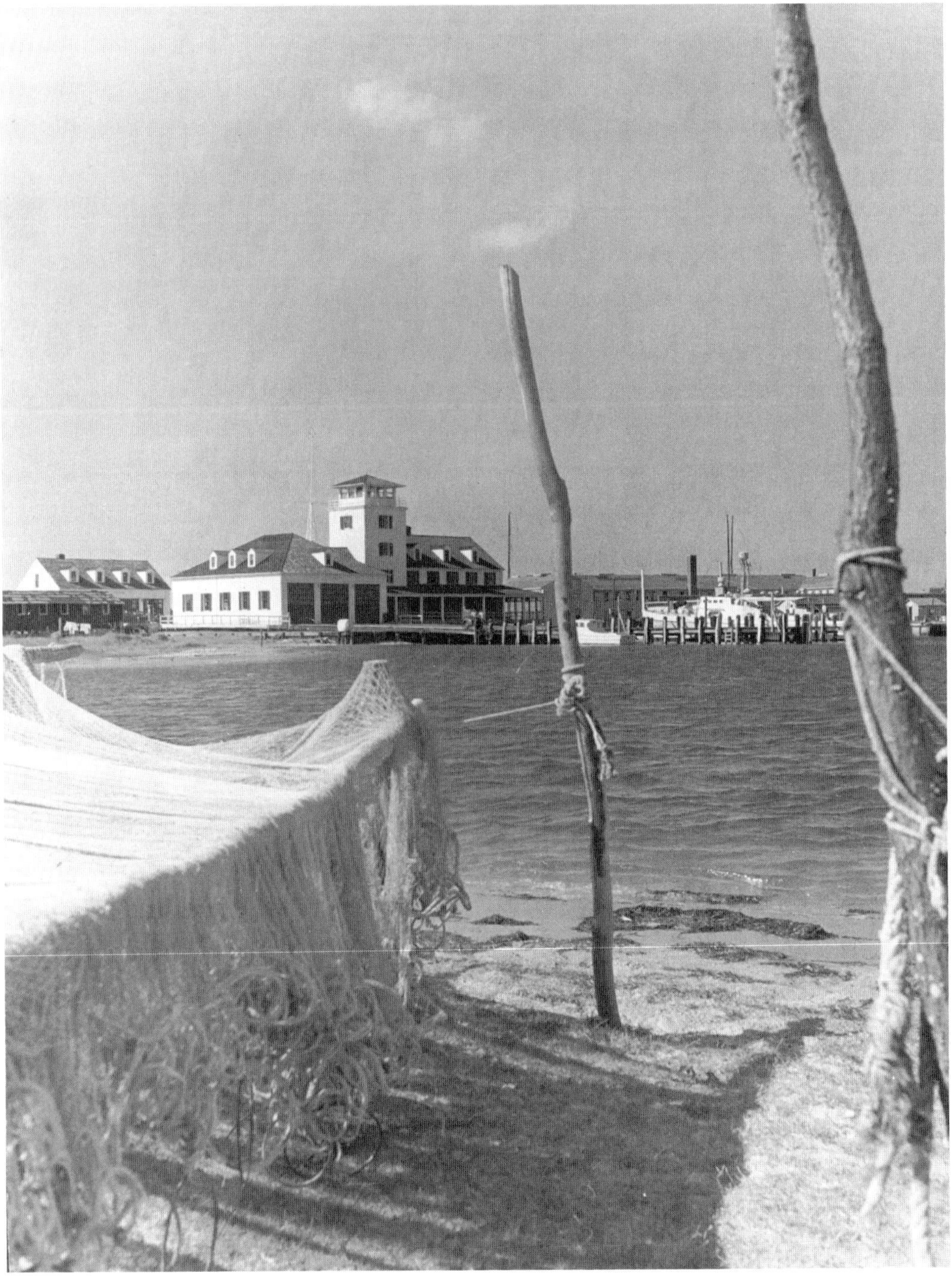

Nets are dried by the fish house across the channel from the Coast Guard station. Others are draped on the fishing boats.

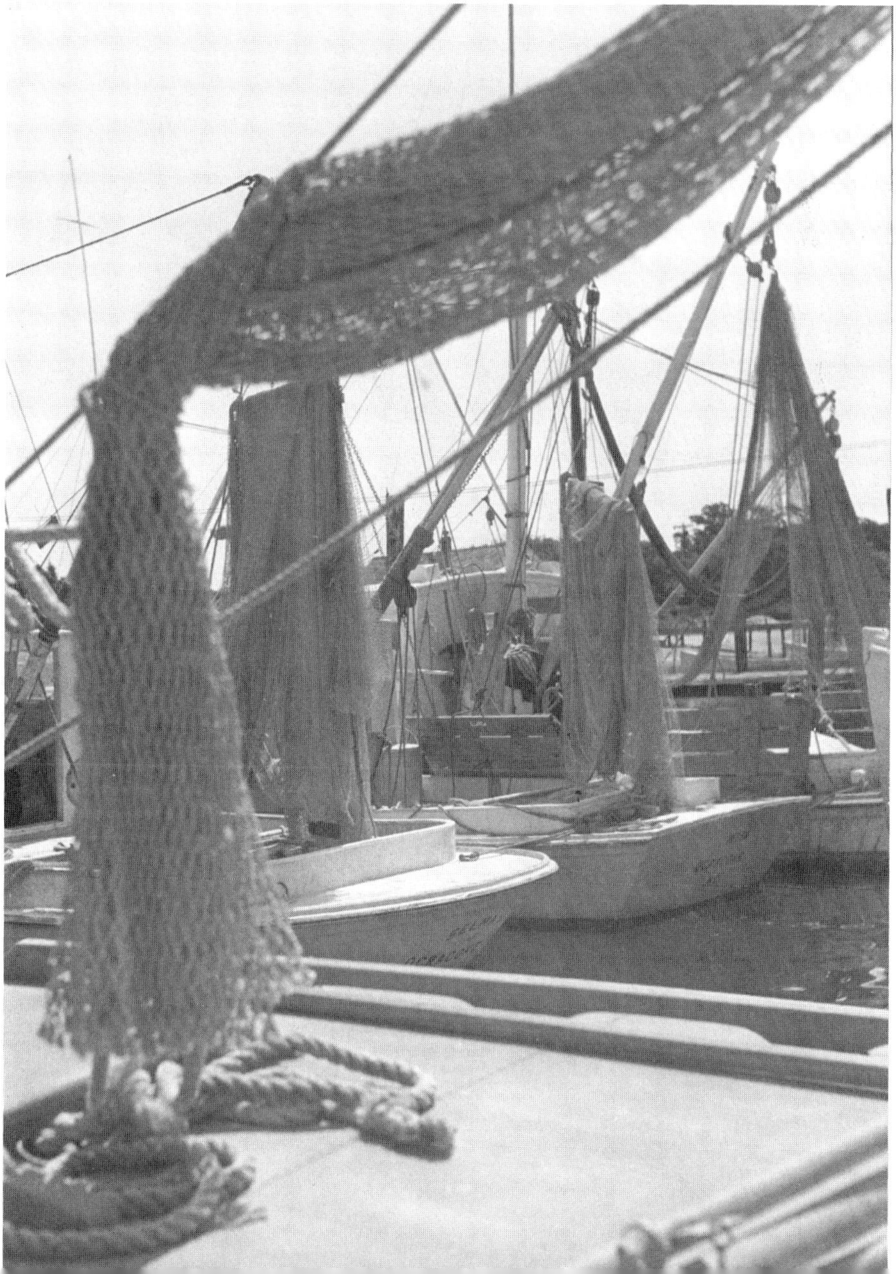

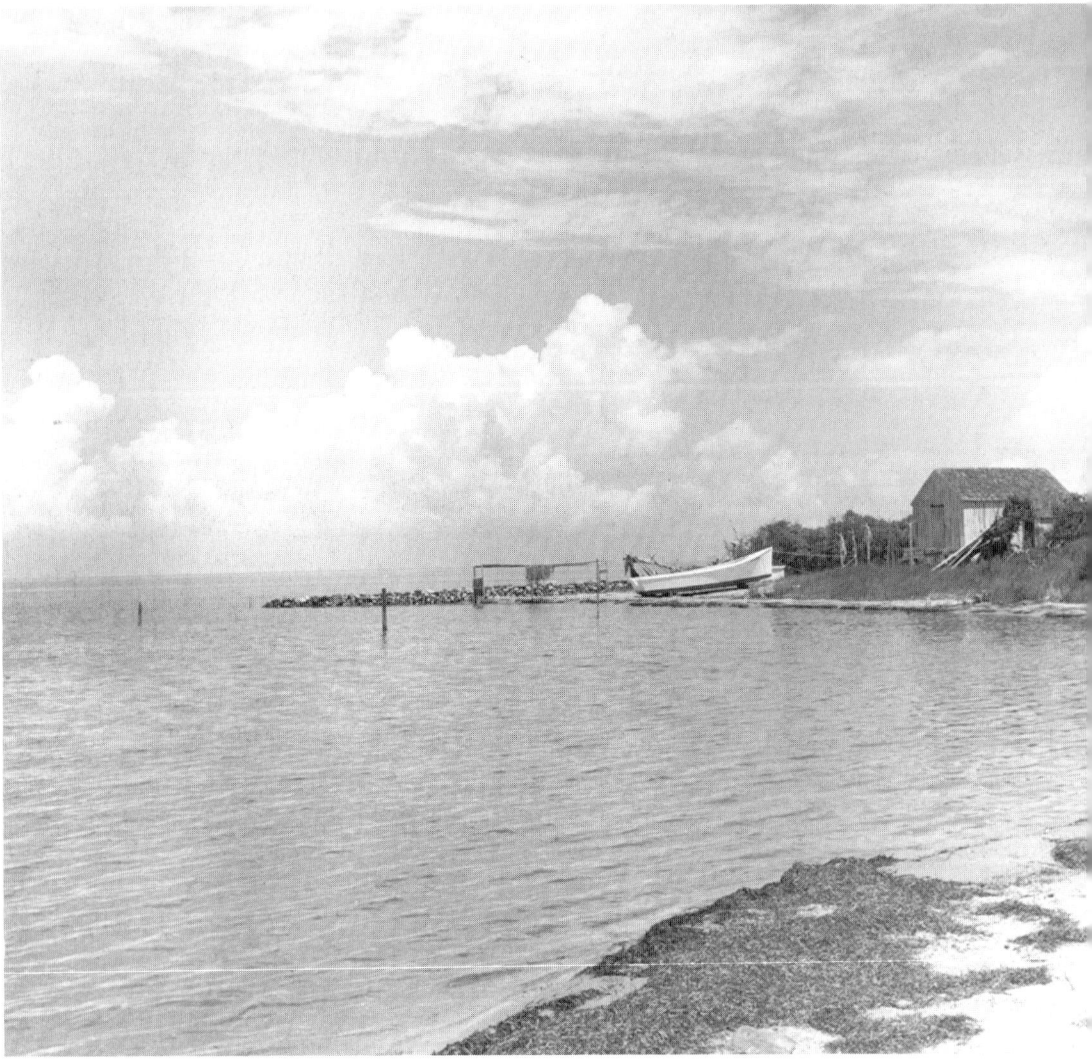

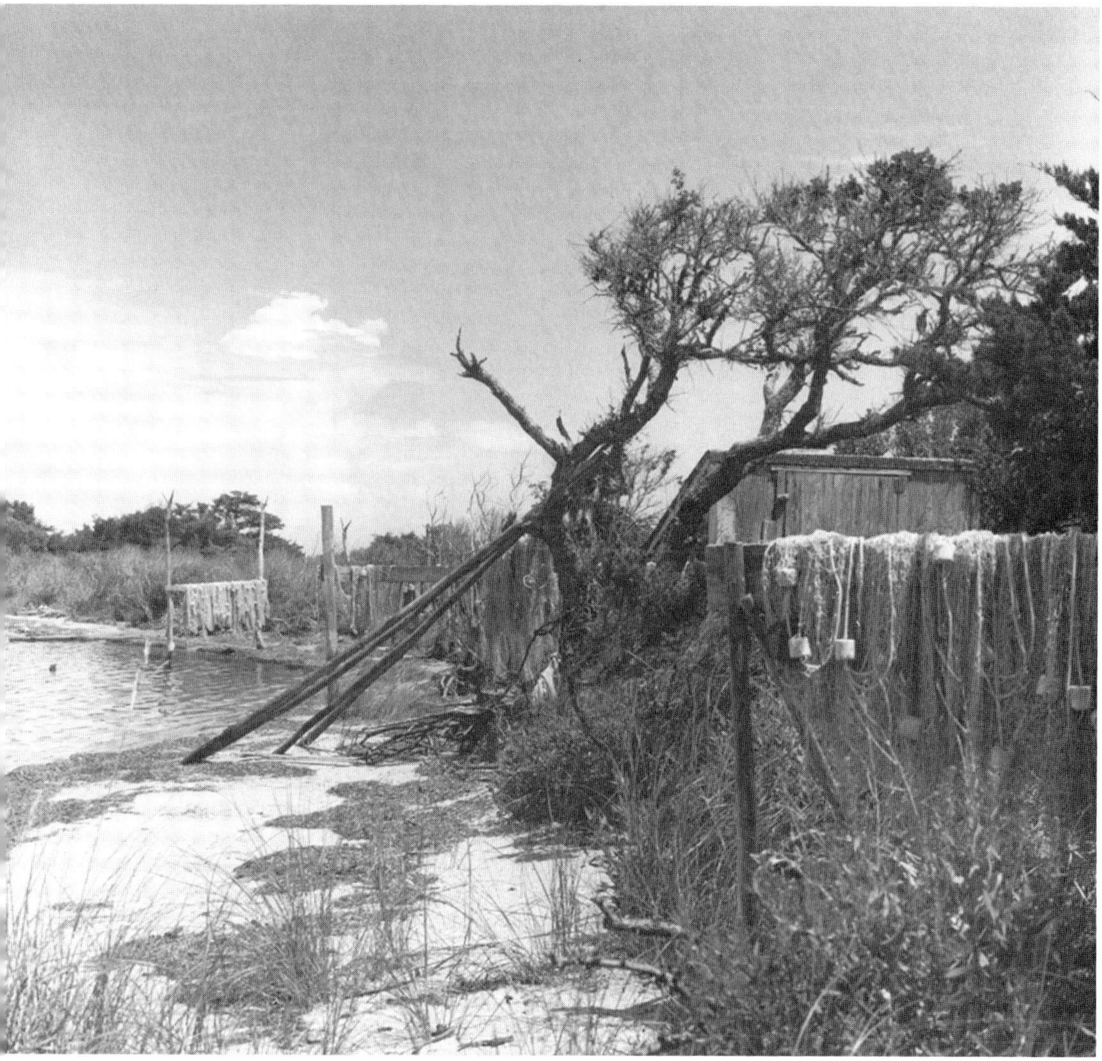

Nets strung out in the sun at Northern Pond

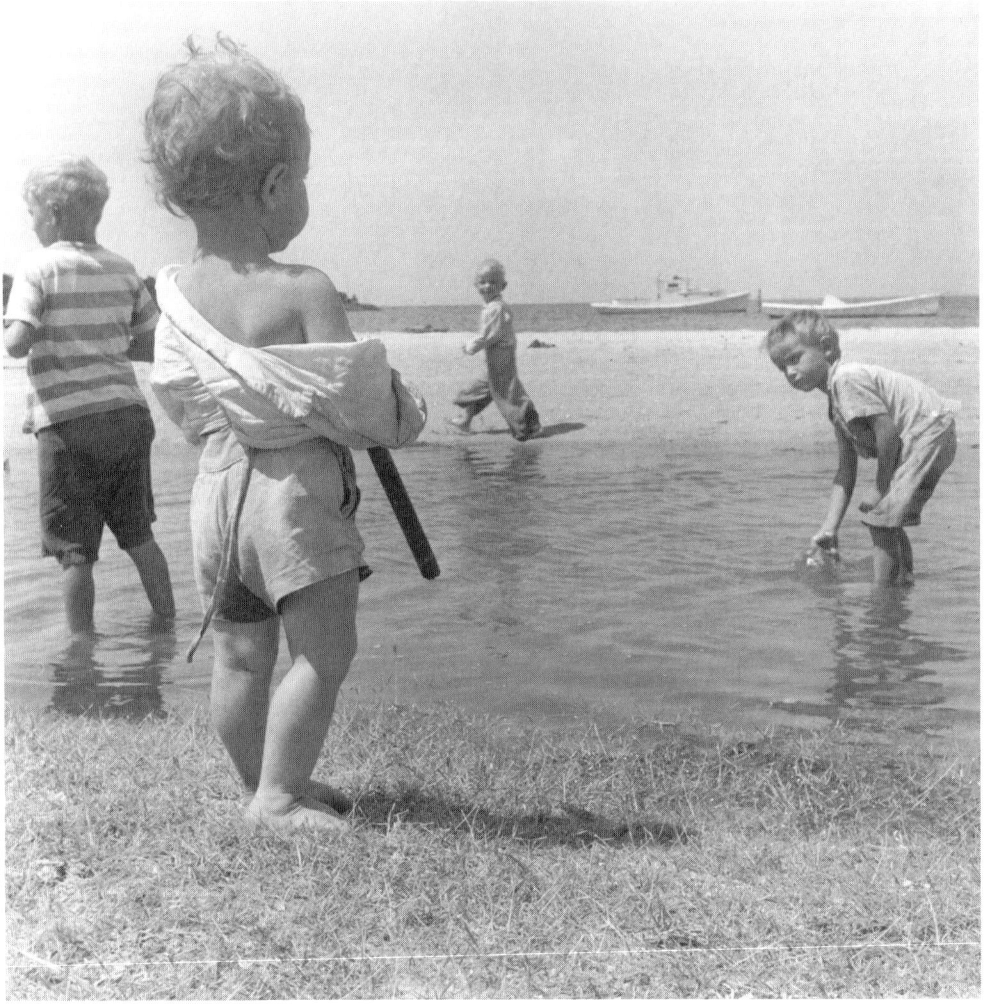

Children play local games improvised in the shallow water among quick, small fish and empty net poles.

Walk north around the point and you will find a world of tangled, gray driftwood, dead trees, and brown seaweed.

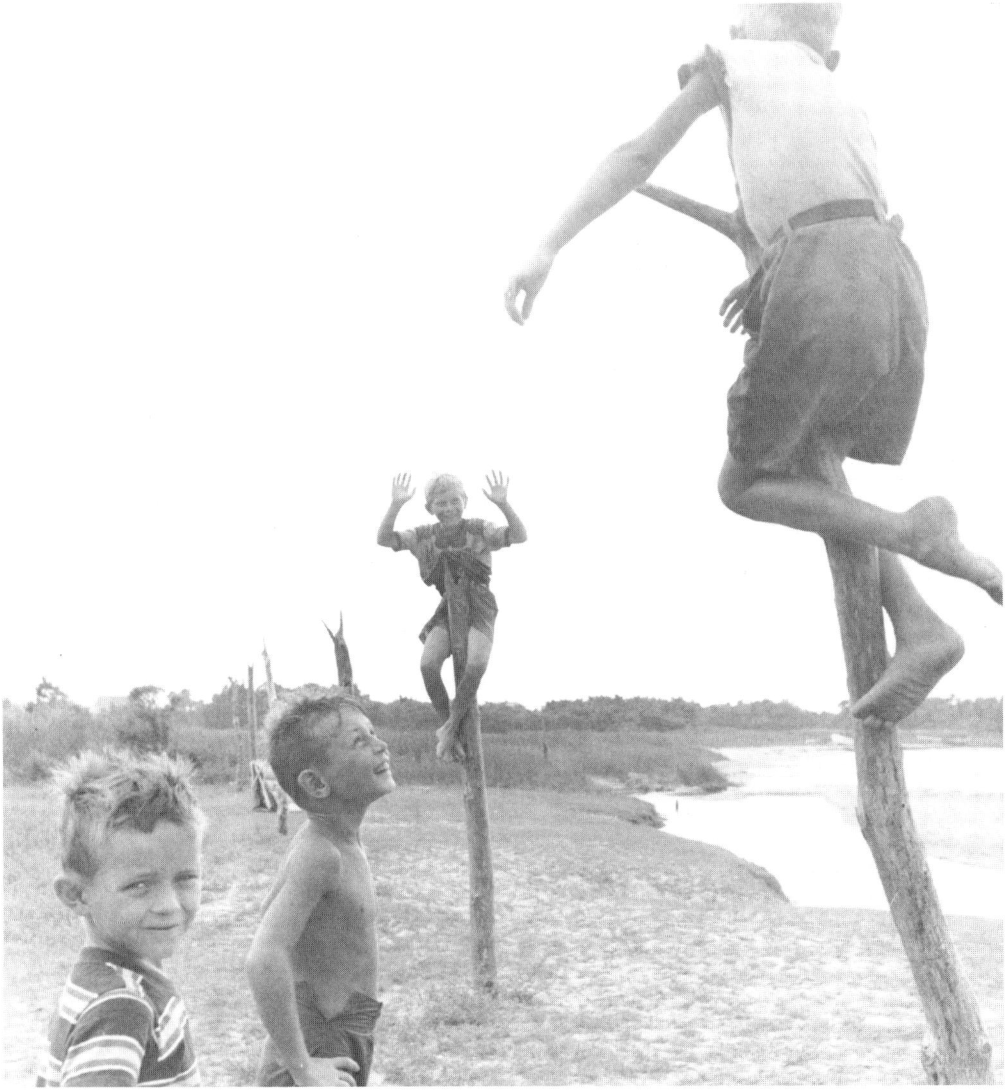

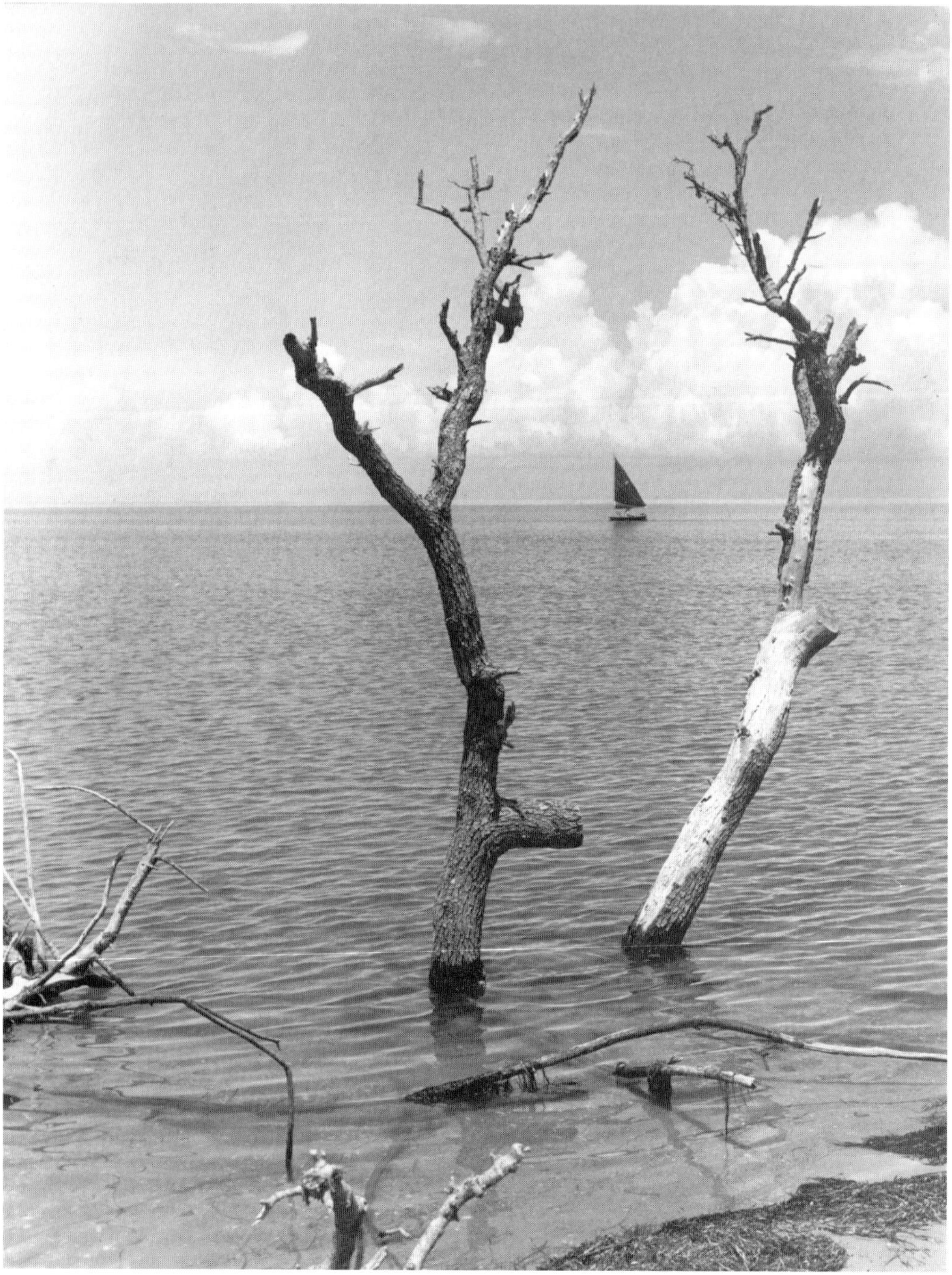

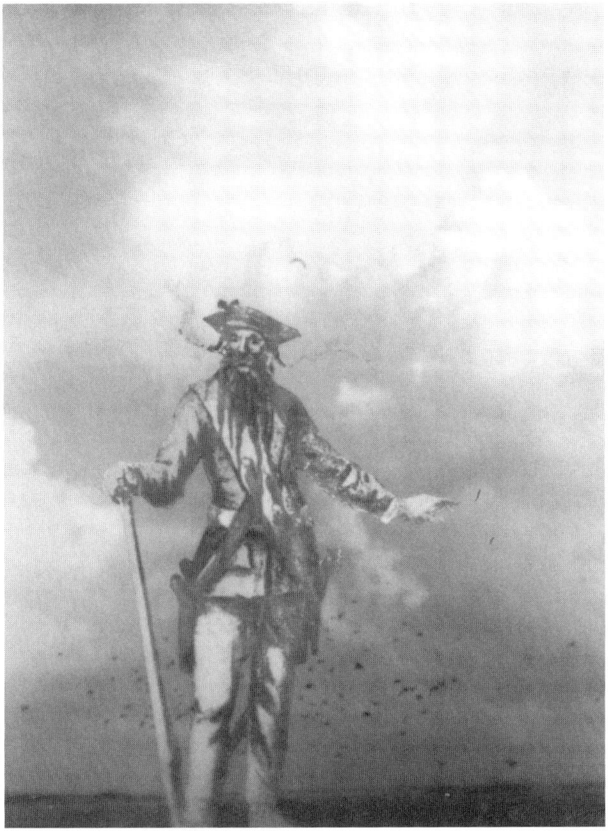

Walk south along the shoreline of the sound from Silver Lake and you will come to Springers Point. Here, Blackbeard the pirate had his headquarters.

His name was Edward Teach, and he was the terror of the Carolina-Virginia coastline in 1717. Fierce, ruthless, delighting in cruelty, he even used his appearance to create terror. He was a strong, broad, hairy man with a long black beard that he braided and tied with ribbons. To improve the effect, he placed under his hat and in his beard slow-burning matches.

He was rumored to have fourteen wives scattered about and was hand-in-glove with North Carolina's governor, Charles Eden. He became such an uncontrolled menace that the people of North Carolina appealed to Governor Alexander Spotswood of Virginia for help. Spotswood replied by dispatching two sloops of shallow draft, able to maneuver in the sound, manned by the crewmen of a British man-o'-war.

On a November morning in 1718, this band engaged and defeated Teach in a bloody battle. The commander, Lieutenant Robert Maynard, took Teach on in single combat, rapier against cutlass. The pirate was wounded twenty-five times before he fell. The victors cut off his head and hung it from the bowsprit by his hair. Wanting sure proof that this bloodstained brute was really done for, they flung his body overboard. Legend says that Teach was so angry and so tough that the body swam seven times around the ship before it gave in and sank. There are even those who claim that it was thirteen times.

Another story credits Teach with giving Ocracoke its name. In the long night before his last battle, he is said to have cried out, "Oh, crow, cock!" to hasten the dawn and high tide, which would allow him to maneuver his ship, the *Adventure*.

But on sixteenth-century maps, the island was called Wokoken, stemming from a tribe called the Woccon. There were many spellings through the years—Woococon, Wococok, Ocock, Ocacoc, and others. All gave way to Ocracoke.

At Springers Point, gaunt trees rise like gallows. An old well marks the site of Teach's lookout tower. Dark English ivy shrouds everything, and the mosquitoes are as ferocious as Blackbeard ever was. Here, you can feel his step from legend into reality.

Teach's buried loot was never found, though treasure hunting still goes on. Teach said, "No one but myself and the devil knows where it is." His treasure remains unfound. His bones lie in the sound off Teach's Hole. Who knows if his ghost walks Ocracoke with the sullen flare of matches burning in its beard?

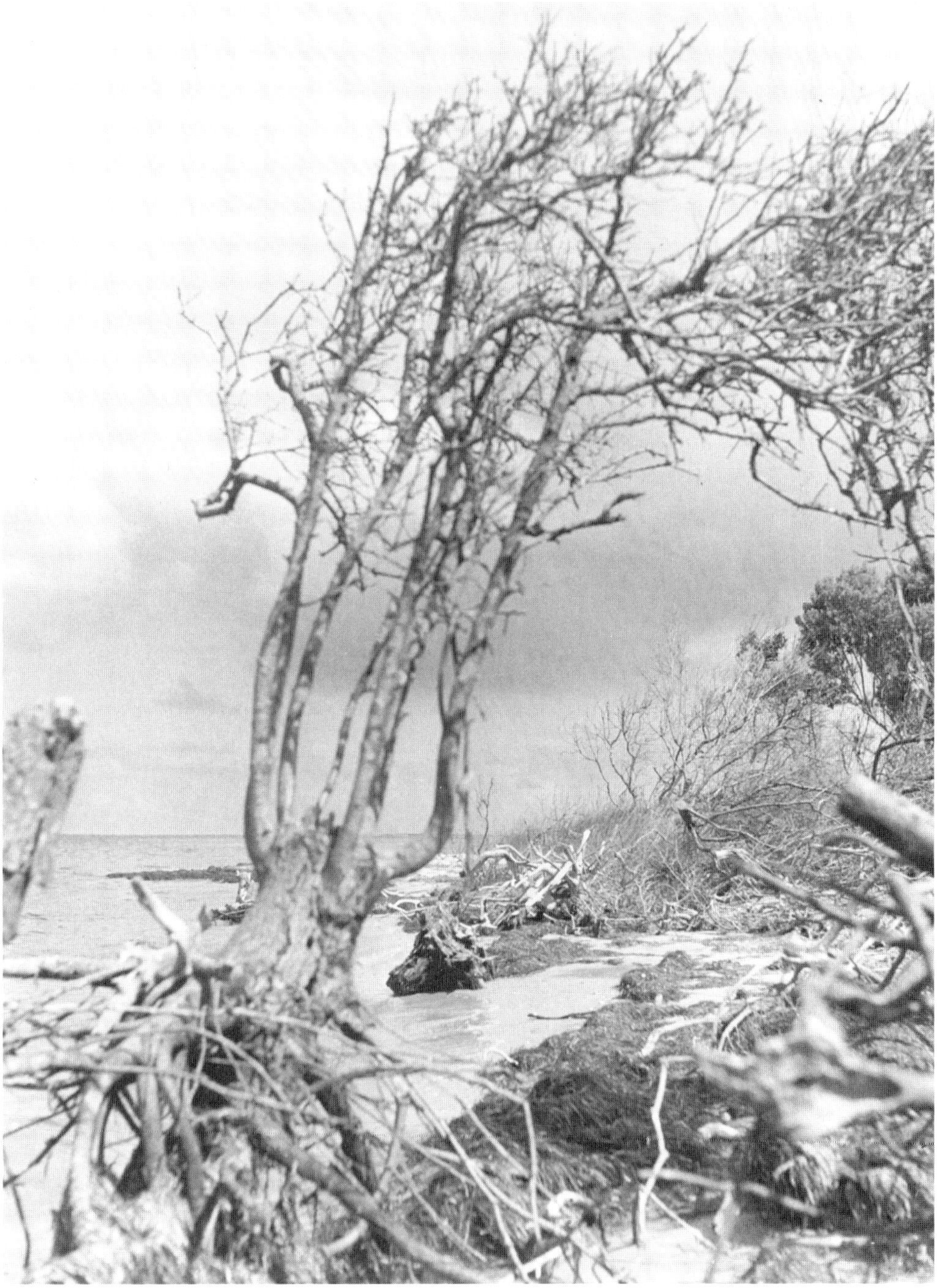

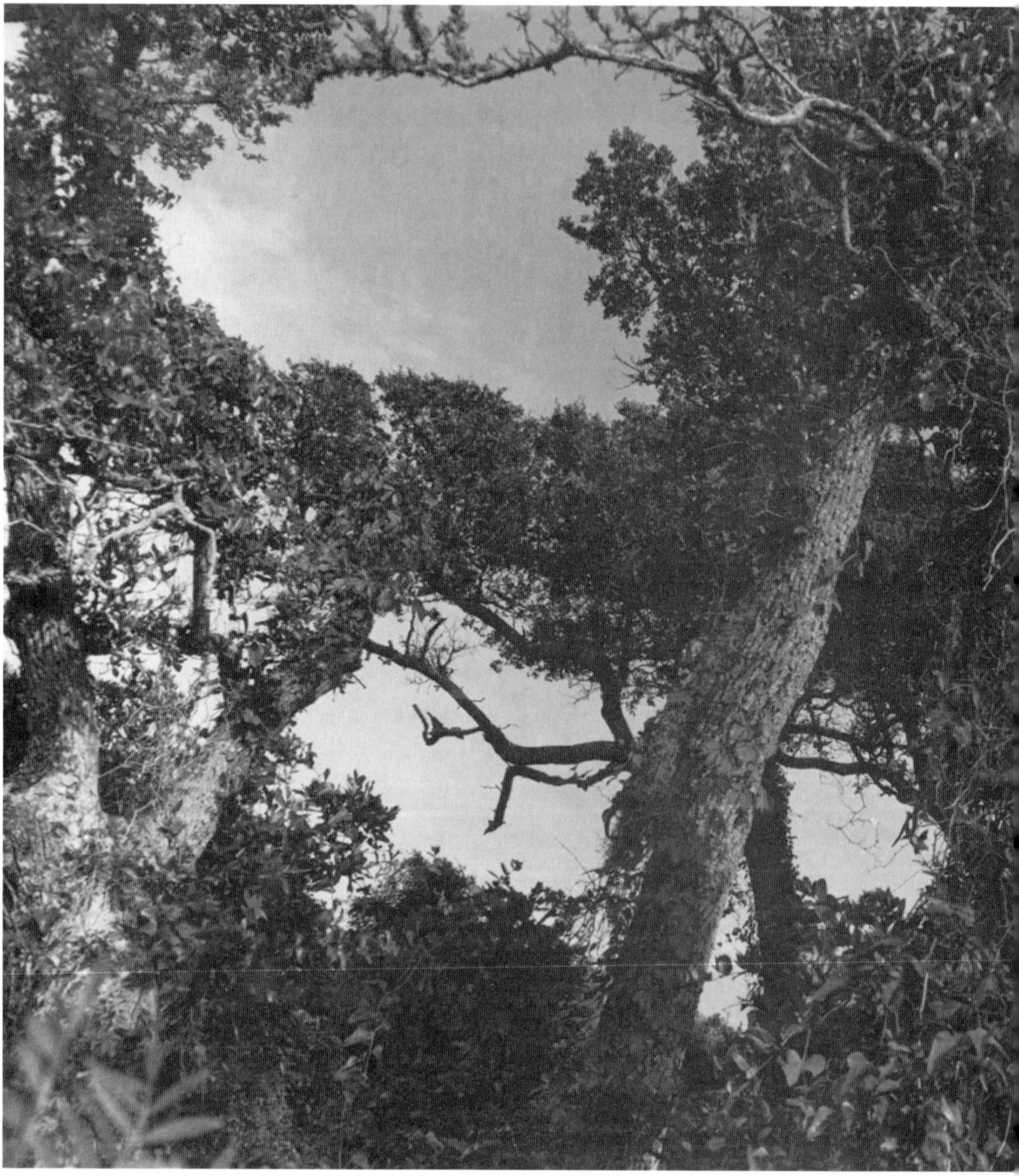

The warped trunks and interlaced branches of the live oaks were here in Blackbeard's time.

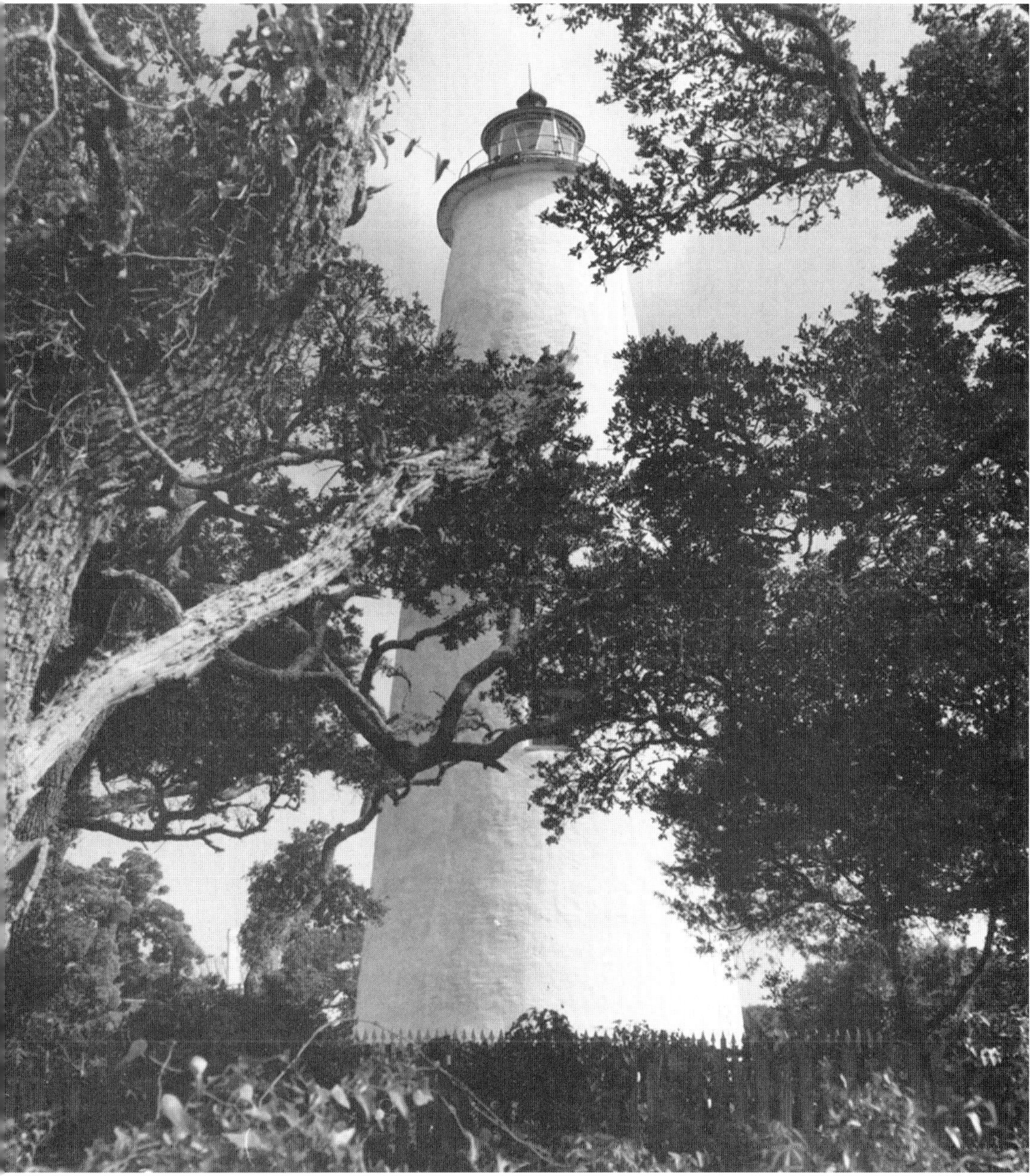

The lighthouse they surround was built 106 years after Blackbeard's body sank beneath the waters of the sound.

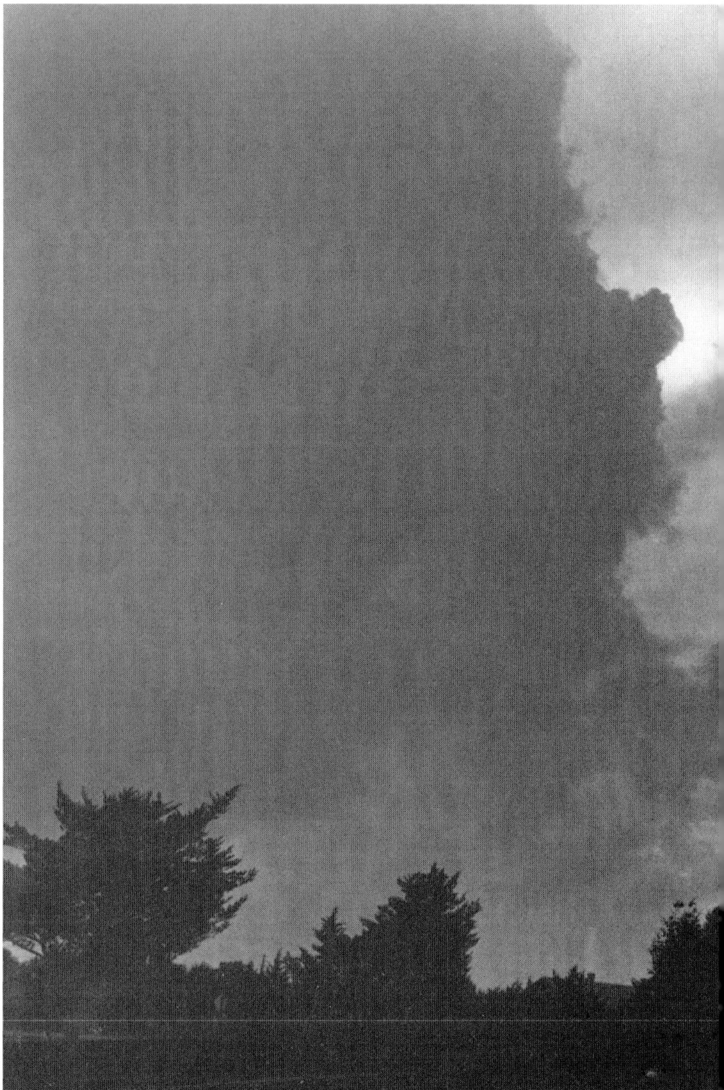

The lighthouse on Ocracoke is the oldest still in operation on the eastern seaboard. Its steady beam can be seen for fourteen miles. The light was first fueled by whale oil, then by kerosene, and now by electricity.

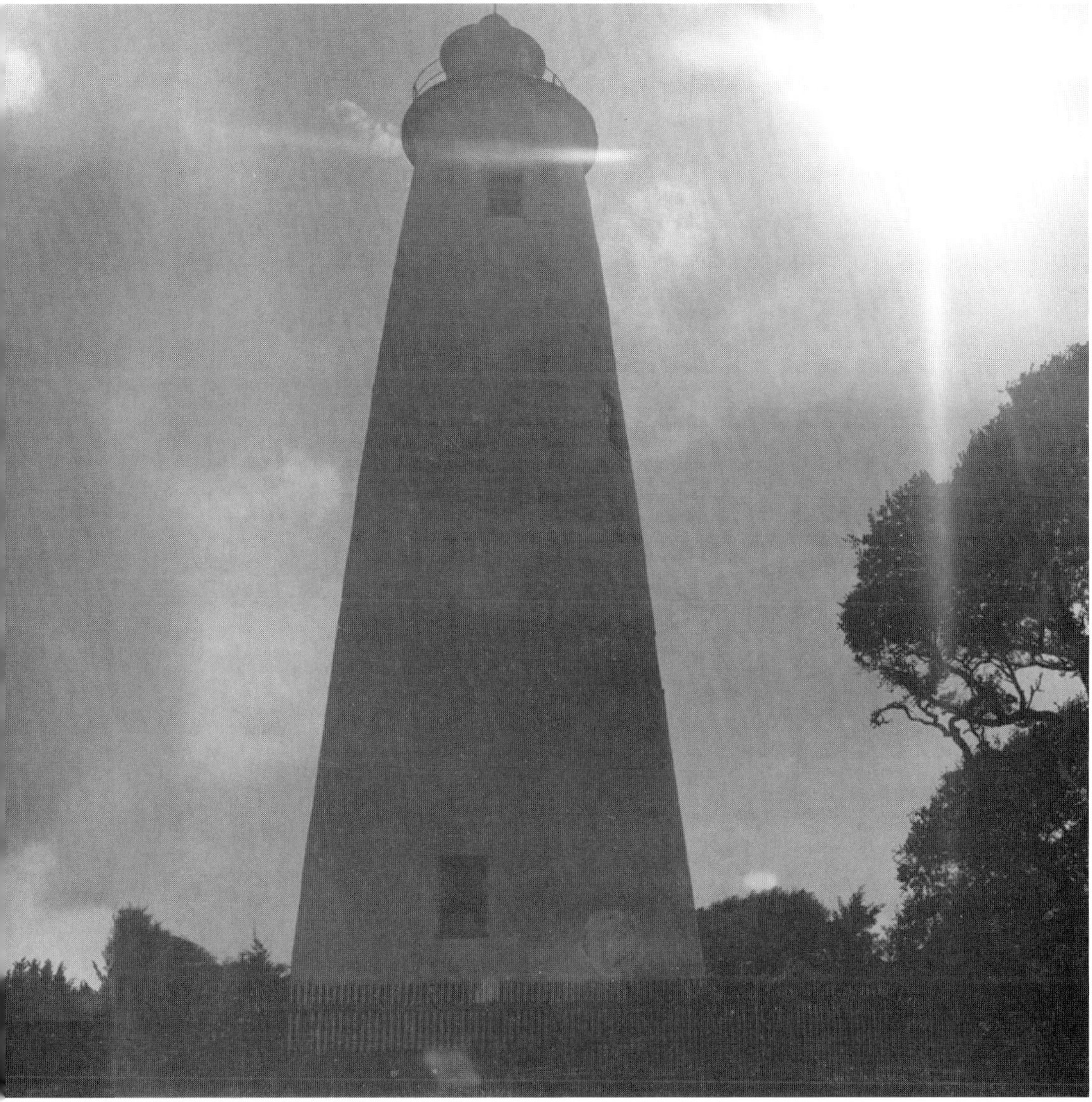

It is not needed today to guide ships as it was in the past, but it is needed for its sense of permanence, for its strong beauty, and as a memory of all the vessels it has kept from disaster. Its light is still a comforting sight.

The first people to live on Ocracoke, the Indians, left no mark on the island but its name. Likewise, the explorers, the settlers, the pirates, the hunters, and the fishermen through the years left little mark on it. Now, the Park Service must preserve the wild beaches.

Some of the residents look doubtfully at the Park Service's new wall of dunes. Wise in the ways of storms,

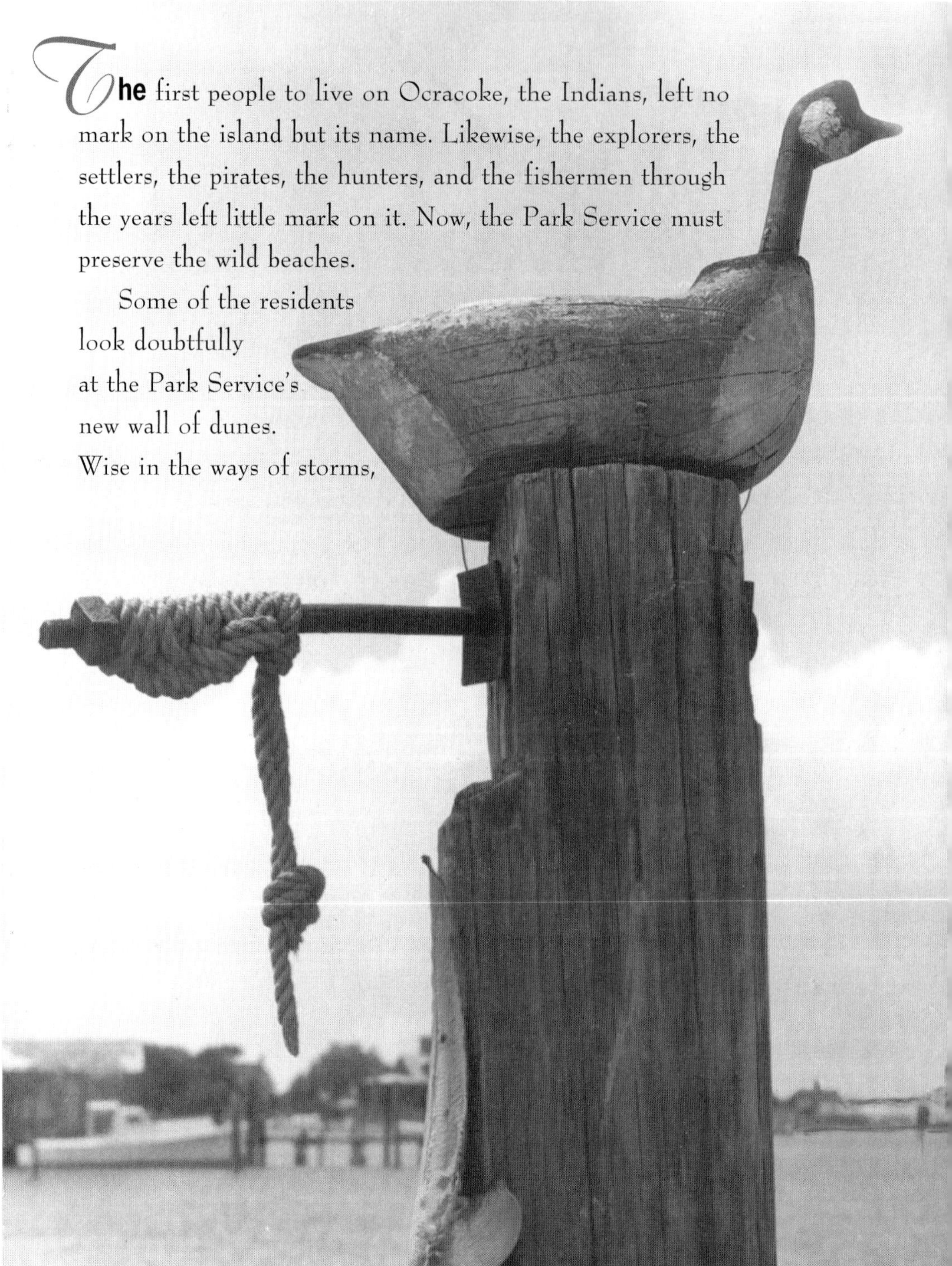

they are afraid that the seawater that once washed harmlessly over the island will be turned back upon them. It will take a bad storm to prove who is right.

With shrimping and commercial fishing on the decline, the people need the steady jobs the Park Service provides, along with the increasing tourist trade, if they are to remain a self-sufficient community.

As Ocracoke moves into the stream of modern life, once-busy Portsmouth, just across the inlet to the south, is now a nearly abandoned ghost town. Despite all of its changes, life here on Ocracoke is still a far cry from the jet age. No one has wanted the island for oil or lumber or power, so it now is a preserve that belongs to all of us and to the people of the future—a distinctive wild landscape rich in history.

Men are modernizing Ocracoke, while other men are trying to preserve it. In the end, the forces of nature will relentlessly shape this wind-swept island. I think it will endure as it always has, and so will its hardy people.

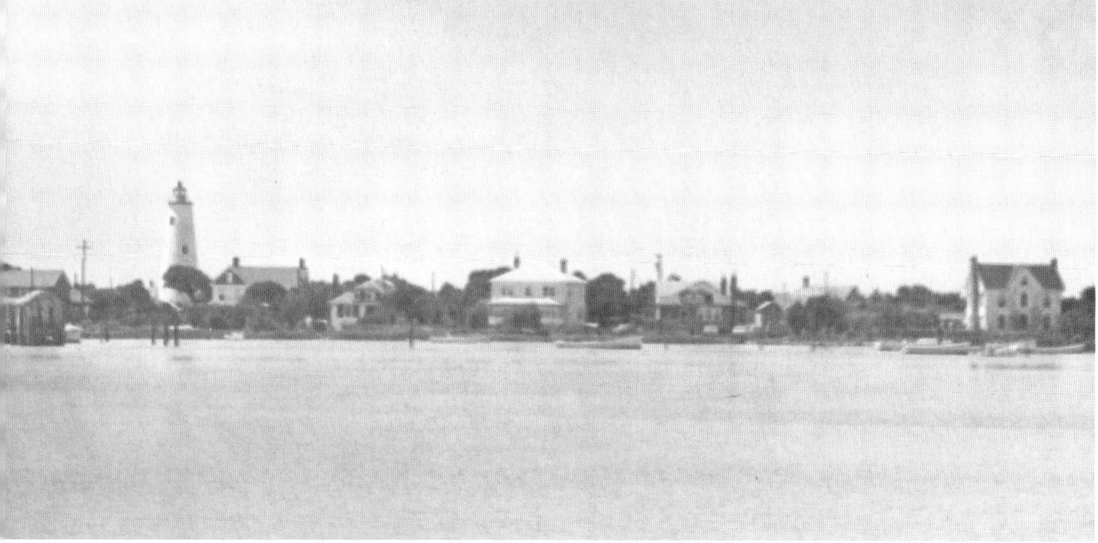

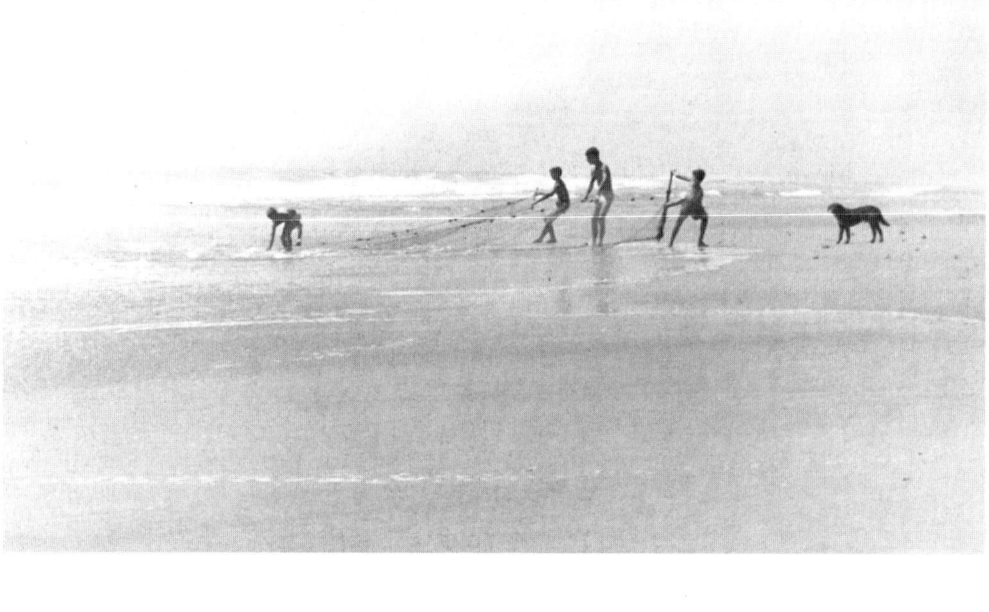